"In *Journey with Jesus through L[...]* ed playbook for serious spiritual [...] it's an inspiring book that can be [...] and thirst for fellowship with Go[...]

"During the season of Lent, the Christian's sense of excitement and anticipation grows more easily as we reimagine the love of God experienced through our prayerful participation in the spiritual disciplines. Prayer, fasting, almsgiving, scriptural study, acts of service, and gratitude all play an integral part in how the community of faith comes together to repent, relive, and renew its commitment to the Risen Christ and the joy of his resurrection power. In this groundbreaking devotional Rev. Dr. Glenn Porter carefully leans upon the testimonial wisdom of Luke's Gospel and his own pastoral experience to offer a practical resource for the modern-day Lenten observer. Whether you are the lead pastor of a church, the head of a Christian education department, or an individual who simply desires to immerse yourself more deeply in the contemplative traditions of the Christian faith, you'll discover that Journey with Jesus through Lent is a timeless resource you can trust as you look to become inspired anew by the radical faith of Jesus during the Lenten season." —Rev. Dr. Christopher Michael Jones, Senior Pastor, First Baptist Church of Hillside, and Visiting Professor of Preaching and Pastoral Administration, New Brunswick Theological Seminary

"*Journey with Jesus through Lent* will challenge your life and strengthen your spirit. Glen Porter's intriguing invitation into the Holy observance of Lent offers a relevant and contemporary understanding of the Lenten tradition through the practical the lens of the African American religious experience." —The Reverend Canon John T. W. Harmon, Rector and Pastor, Trinity Episcopal Church, Washington DC

"Glen Porter's Journey with Jesus through Lent is a brilliant spiritual resource. It is also a practical help for reading the Bible and offers real insight into human experience. I caught myself wanting to read ahead into the next day's lesson." —Rev. Dr. Henry H. Mitchell

"In Journey with Jesus through Lent, Dr. Porter has on offering an important devotional resource for the individual as well as for congregational study. In the "journey" from Ash Wednesday through Resurrection Sunday, the reader is engaged by an academically astute, socially conscious and spiritually challenging work that encourages the reader to reflect and act. As such, this is truly a worthwhile resource for contemplating as well as practicing the themes of the Lenten season." —Rev. Dr. Patrick Jones, Pastor, Bethany Baptist Church, Montpelier, VA and The Center For Lifelong Learning and Leadership (CL3)

"It is with great joy and excitement that I recommend this book to our churches and individuals who want to grow in their faith pilgrimage as Christians. I am personally inspired by this work. As Lent is the journey toward the Passion of our Lord Jesus Christ, this book takes us through all the corners, highways, and sometimes narrow trails, but surely to the great event: the Resurrection!

"In light of the current issues that our country faces today, the book provides a prophetic combination of personal devotions with group discussions, calling us to self-examination and to transformative action. African proverbs and sayings make this magnificent work very much at home both individually and collectively as a Body of Christ. This is a precious tool that God places in our hands, and I will never thank enough our brother, Dr. Glenn Porter, for taking his time to give us this treasure." —Rev. Dr. Eleazar O. Ziherambere, Area Director for Africa/ Director for African American Mission, American Baptist International Ministries

"In every season, one needs, in some way or form, a guide for the journey. Glenn Porter points the way for the Lenten season through a journey with Jesus toward Jerusalem and the cross. With substance, Dr. Porter illuminates the depth of the Spirit and reveals the deep Spirit in substance. The journey takes you from conviction to celebration as you walk with Jesus through prayer, study, meditation, fasting, sacrifice, service, and gratitude. The insightful work will lead your from heartache to hallelujah and I invite all to take the journey." —John Kinney, PhD, Dean, Samuel DeWitt Proctor School of Theology; Senior Vice President, Virginia Union University

"This book is a must read for all those who seek to strengthen their faith and spiritual disciplines by setting aside time for reflection on Jesus Christ, his suffering and his sacrifice, his life, death, burial and resurrection." —Dr. Ervin M. Scott, Pastor, New Rose of Sharon Elim Baptist Church, 55th President, Tidewater Metro Baptist Ministers' Conference of Virginia

"*Journey With Jesus Through Lent* is an inspiring and uplifting ensemble of devotionals. Dr. Porter's epistles of faith, energize the soul and give fresh insight on the redemptive power and ministry of Jesus. Great for personal devotions and for ministry study groups." —Rev. Barbara D. Turner, Second Baptist Church, Roselle, NJ, Christian Writers Ministry

"This book is a must-read for all those who seek to strengthen their faith and spiritual disciplines by setting aside time for reflection on Jesus Christ, his suffering and his sacrifice, his life, death, burial, and resurrection." —Dr. Ervin M. Scott, Pastor, New Rose of Sharon Elim Baptist Church, and 55th President, Tidewater Metro Baptist Ministers' Conference of Virginia

"*Journey with Jesus through Lent* is an inspiring and uplifting ensemble of devotionals. Dr. Porter's epistles of faith energize the soul and give fresh insight on the redemptive power and ministry of Jesus. Great for personal devotions and for ministry study groups." —Rev. Barbara D. Turner, Second Baptist Church, Roselle, NJ, and Christian Writers Ministry

"Dr. Glenn Porter has captured the essence of prayer, devotion, and expectation that characterizes the celebration of the Lenten season. His prolific foundation in the historic tradition coupled with an adept application to today's context makes this devotional an excellent tool for the church and its constituents. Thank you Glenn for this powerful devotional tool!" —Bishop B. Courtney McBath, DMin, Senior Pastor of Calvary Revival Church, Norfolk, VA

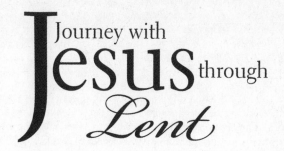

Journey with Jesus through Lent

Glenn E. Porter Sr.
Foreword by Benjamin Greene Jr.

JUDSON PRESS
PUBLISHERS SINCE 1824

Join our mailing list for updates and special offers.

www.judsonpress.com/mailing_list.cfm

Journey with Jesus through Lent
© 2017 by Judson Press, Valley Forge, PA 19482-0851
All rights reserved.

Judson Press has made every effort to trace the ownership of all quotes. In the event of a question arising from the use of a quote, we regret any error made and will be pleased to make the necessary correction in future printings and editions of this book.

Unless otherwise indicated, Scripture quotations in this volume are from the New Revised Standard Version Bible, copyright 1989, Division of Christian Education of the National Council of the Churches of Christ in the United States of America. Used by permission. All rights reserved.

Scriptures marked GNT are from the *Good News Translation*. Copyright © 1992 by American Bible Society. Used by permission. MSG are from THE MESSAGE. Copyright © 1993, 1994, 1995. Used by permission of NavPress Publishing Group. KJV are from *The Holy Bible*, King James Version. Public domain. AMP are from the *Amplified Bible, Old Testament*. Copyright © 1962, 1964 by Zondervan Publishing House. Used by permission. Moffatt are from *The Bible: A New Translation* by James Moffatt. Copyright 1954 by James Moffatt. Reprinted by permission of Harper & Row, Publishers, Inc.

Interior design by Wendy Ronga/Hampton Design Group.
Cover design by Lisa Delgado/Delgado and Company, Inc.

Library of Congress Cataloging-in-Publication data
Names: Porter, Glenn E., author. Title: Journey with Jesus through Lent / Glenn E. Porter Sr. Description: Judson Press, Valley Forge, PA: Judson Press, 2017. Identifiers: LCCN 2016031900 (print) | LCCN 2016034565 (ebook) | ISBN 9780817017774 (pbk.: alk. paper) | ISBN 9780817081676 (e-book) Subjects: LCSH: Lent—Meditations. | Lent—Prayers and devotions—English. | African Americans—Prayers and devotions. | African American public worship. | Bible. Luke—Meditations. | Church year meditations. Classification: LCC BV85 .P585 2017 (print) | LCC BV85 (ebook) | DDC 242/.34—dc23 LC record available at https://lccn.loc.gov/2016031900

Printed in the U.S.A.
First printing, 2017.

For my beloved wife and inspiration,

Lisa Gayle

Contents

Foreword

I am grateful for the privilege of writing the Foreword to Glen Porter's resource *Journey with Jesus through Lent*. I want to commend Rev. Dr. Porter for the challenge he gives us by investigating, discovering, and sharing the acts of Jesus during the days leading up to his crucifixion and resurrection. Born from Porter's experiences as a broadcaster, print journalist, college professor and pastor, this volume invites the reader to come along as he explores how Jesus' journey can help us recapture a commitment to justice and act as catalysts for change.

Many pastors, congregations, and communities are tired and discouraged. The heavenly vision of the people of God, following their Master in pouring out life for the good of all, grows dim. Paying the bills, adding a few members, and maintaining the building seem to be tedious tasks. The anxieties of mere survival that are characteristic of modern society are mirrored in our churches. Living amid the meaningless and empty chatter often fueled by 24-hour news cycles, mindless entertainment, the drama of family, work, or community (or the lack thereof), we find ourselves searching for more—more substance, more meaning, more hope. *Journey with Jesus through Lent* invites the reader to step aside and discover a better way to live.

People throughout the country are afraid of people who are different from them. Porter believes the values and skills of conciliation can help break down walls that divide people, communities, and nations. For renewal to take hold there must be a redefinition of relationship. He encourages us to talk honestly and openly with each other, to listen and to move actively, to facilitate coalition building, and restore confidence that people can make a difference. There must be newness within our lives and within the church, if we are to live.

Porter illustrates how justice issues continue to affect our communities today. These serious realities run the gamut from the closing of businesses, industries, and hospitals to the challenges of an aging community; from the decreasing quality of education to the lack of adequate housing and rising unemployment; from the continued pain of drug and alcohol addiction to the influence of hate groups. While they may differ in feature and scope, in many instances, these issues resemble those Jesus confronted on his way to the crucifixion.

I hear Porter urging, "Get on board. Get on board!" He highlights that we are not called simply to identify the social, economic, psychological, and political injustices that impact our individual lives and the life of the local congregation today. He moves us to a sense of urgency to become God's agents of change and offers this Lenten study as a road map out of the wilderness. To become effective, we need to begin with the realities of the present and effect change by moving from the sacred page into action.

Journey with Jesus through Lent steps in and provides a much-needed Lenten devotional for African American congregations. For individuals, these pages fill the need for those who hunger for a biblical, practical, thoughtful, transforming, and scholarly process that will assist them in spiritual growth. For pastors, the book offers rich content for a congregational-wide seasonal study. Using a combination of personal devotional and small-group study formats, the book features weekday devotions to challenge individual readers to advance their individual faith by following in Jesus' footsteps, and each week's Sunday meditation reinforces individual progress through group participation.

Each week focuses on a different spiritual discipline: prayer, fasting, almsgiving, study, service, and gratitude. Porter goes beyond the traditional benefits of these historic disciplines, which help believers to find the clarity and strength to resist temptation and to experience forgiveness and regeneration. He develops a movement that enables readers to internalize a vision of hope, to share the vision with one another in the congregation, and to disseminate their vision into the surrounding community. Along the way, God's people learn to take charge of their lives and create a new community of faith, together.

Journey with Jesus through Lent is a valuable resource for pastors, Christian educators, and congregations alike, with its eloquent and succinct storytelling and its powerfully prophetic message. Taking Luke's Gospel for its biblical foundation, the devotional study offers concise, readable, and relevant inspiration. The meditations in this uplifting work bring together Christian faith and African wisdom for grappling with critical issues confronting God's people today.

Benjamin Greene Jr.
Vice President
American Baptist Extension Corporation

Acknowledgments

There are so many people for whom I am grateful. Without their assistance, support, guidance, and wisdom, this project would never have come to fruition. I'm deeply appreciative to friends, teaching colleagues, and brothers and sisters in ministry.

I'm indebted to Reverend Jonathan L. Pemberton, my son in ministry and my pastoral assistant at Queen Street Baptist Church. Jonathan aptly upped his administrative and pastoral responsibilities for me during August 2015 and again in February 2016 so that I could truly devote the necessary attention to "looking out the window" and writing.

I acknowledge with gratitude those whom God has placed in my pastoral care, over thirty years: Mount Zion Baptist Church (Staunton, VA), Gillfield Baptist Church (Petersburg, VA), and the Essex and North New Jersey associations of American Baptist Churches of New Jersey. I'm particularly and enormously grateful for the loving congregation that my family and I call our church home: Queen Street Baptist Church. And of course, I'm always grateful for Second Baptist Church (Roselle, NJ), where I first met the Lord. To my students and colleagues at Tidewater Community College, thank you for teaching me so many lessons in and out of the classroom. It's a joy!

I've got to say thank you to my family circle—Parker, Briggs, and Porter—for steadfast willingness to support consistently the ministries to which God has entrusted to my stewardship. And thank you, John Walker, for being a friend.

Tremendous appreciation is expressed for my new friends at the Williamsburg Christian Center for providing me a sacred place and space to retreat and write.

Thank you to the gifted Judson Press team for supporting this project and walking me along this new journey, particularly: Laura Alden, Rev. Rebecca Irwin-Diehl, Lisa Blair, Linda Johnson-LeBlanc, and Gale Tull.

Thank you to my loving and sacrificial family—Lisa, and our three sons, Glenn Eugene Jr., Luke Proctor, and Adam DeWitt; your unwavering support is always a source of encouragement.

Finally I thank God.

Introduction

Lent—known as *Tessarakosti* in Greek and *Quadragesima* in Latin, for "the Forty"[1]—is the period of the Christian liturgical calendar that pointedly directs believers to the redemptive works of Jesus Christ. It's the reflective prelude to the two most important celebrations on the church calendar—Good Friday and Easter. Lent prepares us for the crucifixion and resurrection of Jesus Christ.

It was after the Emperor Constantine called the first ecumenical discussions at the Council of Nicea in 325 that the length of Lent became forty days.[2] The number 40 is familiar in biblical literature. In Genesis 7, the Lord sends rain "on the earth forty days and forty nights," causing the great flood that wipes out everyone, except Noah and his family and whatever they loaded onto the ark. In Exodus, we witness Israel wandering in the wilderness for forty years, in which time they feast on miracle meals provided by God. Moses fasted for forty days and nights (Exodus 34:28; Deuteronomy 9:9). In 1 Kings 19, the prophet Elijah is running fearfully from Jezebel, King Ahab's wife, because she has threatened to have him killed. Elijah is resting under a broom tree, when an angel of the Lord speaks to him and inspires him to get up and get going. "He got up, and ate and drank; then he went in the strength of that food forty days and forty nights to Horeb the mount of God" (1 Kings 19:8). After Jonah's reluctant prophetic intervention, the Ninevites fasted forty days and nights (Jonah 3:4). And the Gospels of Matthew and Luke both record that Jesus fasted for forty days in the wilderness.

It's unclear if the early church's original pre-Easter period of fasting was limited to new Christian converts preparing for baptism, or the entire church. The first-century ecclesial handbook, the *Didache* (pronounced "Did-ah-Kay"), is unclear. However, the *Didache* instructs:

> (And) prior to the baptism,
> [1] let the one baptizing fast;
> [2] and let the one being baptized.
> [3] and if any others have the strength,
> [let them fast also].[3]

As a ritual surrounding the process for baptismal candidates, the fast could have lasted one, two, or three days, or even forty hours—in observance of what was believed to be the duration of Christ's time in the tomb. At any rate, it eventually encompassed the whole church.

How churches counted the forty days varied, depending on location. The East fasted on weekdays, while the Western church observance was shorter but included Saturdays. Both places practiced a strict celebration that included fasting. This prohibited consumption of any meat or animal products, including fish. Gregory the Great (540–604) is credited with establishing many of our current Western traditions, including the establishment and naming of Ash Wednesday and securing the 40 days of Lent (which exclude Sundays). *Christian History* magazine, in an article titled "The Beginning of Lent," describes the early ceremony practiced on Ash Wednesday:

> As Christians came to the church for forgiveness, Gregory marked their foreheads with ashes reminding them of the biblical symbol of repentance (sackcloth and ashes) and mortality: "You are dust, and to dust you will return" (Gen. 3:19).[4]

While during Lent attention is given to individual self-examination, penitence, devotion, and renewal, some churches interpret the season as a communal practice, with great emphasis on the community fast. Trinity United Church of Christ in Chicago, Illinois, conducts a church-wide fast during the Lenten season. For 2015, its theme was "Renew, Reclaim, Restore, Reconnect—Renewing our relationship with God, Reclaiming our African heritage, Restoring justice and mercy, and Reconnecting to our community."[5] The church explained the biblical foundation for fasting, as well as offering three types of fasts: fasting to confront destructive forces; the Daniel Fast; and abstaining from certain foods or items.[6]

For Protestants in North America, Lent's forty days begin on Ash Wednesday and continue through Holy Week. Ash Wednesday is a day of penitence. Palms saved from the previous Palm Sunday are burned, then mixed with a little water (like tears) or oil. On Ash Wednesday, Christians attend church, and a minister uses the ashes to make a small cross on believers' foreheads. The smudged cross is a personal reminder and public testimony of Jesus' salvific love and forgiveness.

We're witnessing an increasing number of African American congregations who are including Ash Wednesday worship services in their annual calendars. The historic Alfred Street Baptist Church in Washington, DC, has celebrated the distribution of ashes for three years. Senior Pastor Dr. Howard-John Wesley says many people were curious when he shared his vision of the imposition of ashes on Ash Wednesday. "It is important to remember that much of what we do in Christian Protestantism, even though not fully acknowledged, is shaped and influenced by our Catholic roots."[7] He adds, "In Catholicism, the distribution of ashes is not a sacrament, meaning the ashes themselves are not a means of receiving grace."[8]

Wesley is suggesting that both Catholicism and Protestantism can view the imposition of ashes as a "memorial" of Lent. Sundays, designated for the celebration of corporate worship, are not calculated in the forty days. Two weeks in Lent are given special significance: Passion Week and Holy Week. Passion Week begins with Passion Sunday, which is two weeks before Easter, and continues to Palm Sunday eve. Holy Week extends from Palm Sunday (one week before Easter) to Easter eve. The special days in Holy Week are Palm Sunday, Maundy Thursday, and Good Friday.

Palm Sunday commemorates Jesus' triumphal, yet humble, arrival into Jerusalem, recorded in all four Gospels: Luke 19:28-40; Matthew 21:1-9; Mark 11:1-10; and John 12:12-18. Maundy Thursday observes the biblical accounts of Jesus sharing the Passover meal with his disciples (Luke 22:19-20) and subsequently washing the disciples' feet. From this episode we get the ordinance of the Lord's Supper.

Good Friday is the observance of the suffering and death of Jesus. Within many African American congregations, the Good Friday worship service features seven sermons based on the seven expressions attributed to Jesus during his crucifixion. The order is generally

1. Father, forgive them; for they do not know what they are doing (Luke 22:34).
2. Truly I tell you, today you will be with me in Paradise (Luke 23:43).
3. "Woman, here is your son." Then he said to the disciple, "Here is your mother" (John 19:26-27).
4. And about three o'clock Jesus cried with a loud voice, "Eli, Eli, lema sabachthani?" that is, "My God, my God, why have you forsaken me?" (Matthew 27:46 and Mark 15:34).
5. I am thirsty (John 19:28).
6. It is finished (John 19:28).
7. Father, into your hands I commend my spirit (Luke 23:46).

Introduction

The "Seven Last Words" or "Seven Last Expressions" worship service is often a black church community event. For example, Second Calvary Baptist Church in Norfolk, Virginia, has hosted a "Seven Last Words of Christ on the Cross" service for almost thirty years. Host pastor Dr. Geoffrey Guns invites local ministers to preach the sermons. The guest pastors bring their congregations, and the Second Calvary sanctuary is filled with several hundred enthusiastic worshippers who look forward to the annual service, which can last three hours. Because of its soaring popularity in Hampton Roads, and Pastor Guns's evangelistic zeal, Second Calvary in 2014 added a second service that begins at 7 p.m., targets the Millennial worshipper, and features young or "emerging" preachers.

Services traditionally begin at noon, a reminder of the time in which Jesus was crucified. While the liturgical color for Lent is purple (featured in church paraments and clergy stoles), the one exception is Good Friday, whose color is black, signifying death. Some congregations strip their pulpits and lecterns of any colorful paraments, leaving the sanctuary bare. This helps emphasize an atmosphere of contrition, remorse, and self-denial.

How to Use This Book

This Lenten devotional is designed as a seasonal resource for congregational, family, or personal use. It's presented through the eyes of an African American Baptist pastor and college professor, and therefore is most appropriately suited for the black church. The issues, stories, illustrations, quotes, and concerns are offered through the uniqueness and particularities of my black experience—rooted in fertile African soil and growing in the era of the grassroots "Black Lives Matter" movement, at a time of an unrelenting twenty-four-hour news cycle and social media feeds that are advancing, in real time, unbelievable episodes of brutality and violence inflicted upon persons of color, and the most vulnerable. Moreover, my theological perspective has been shaped by my seminary professors and colleagues at my alma mater, the Samuel DeWitt Proctor School of Theology at Virginia Union University.

Utilizing the Gospel of Luke as the biblical foundation, the meditations lead the reader through the spiritual themes of repentance and preparation for sharing in the death and resurrection of Christ. Why Luke's account? There is a palpable radicalism and universalism that leaps from the pages of the Gospel According to Luke. Jesus' message was initially rejected by his own hometown people in Nazareth, and then sent "into all the world" for the salvation of all people, Jews and Gentiles. His point of view unapologetically weds Jesus with a powerful and controversial social gospel movement.

The journey picks up as the Galilean section of the Lukan narrative closes. With Luke 9:51, Jesus is destined for Jerusalem. Contextually, the disciples have failed to grasp truly the identity and message of Jesus. They are bickering "as to which one of them was the greatest" (Luke 9:46). They don't truly understand his message of salvation and social reversal. And so, the narrative begins with Jesus advancing God's purpose of salvation for humanity. The misunderstanding and rejection that surrounded and accompanied Jesus' initial sermon (Luke 4:16-30) continues, even now, as "he set his face to go to Jerusalem." With each daily meditation, the reader is following in the footsteps of Jesus.

The book consists of seven weeks of meditations, including Bible readings for Holy Week. The first week begins on Wednesday because Ash Wednesday is the start of Lent. The chapters open with a theme for the week. Each day begins with a Scripture reading and an African proverb or other saying, followed by a meditation. Unlike most Lenten devotionals, this work provides readings for every day throughout the season, including Sundays. Each devotion concludes with a scriptural prayer focus.

Introduction

The Sunday meditations have Group Discussion questions for use in church school, Bible study, or a spiritual renewal retreat. It's a practical and user-friendly resource for the local church. Additionally, a weekly Personal Action section challenges the reader to utilize the spiritual discipline for a transformed life.

It's my earnest prayer that these devotions—this journey—will strengthen you in your faith pilgrimage. Let the Lord speak to you, to your heart. Truly, the journey can become the destination.

Notes

1. Nicholas V. Russo, "The Early History of Lent," The Center for Christian Ethics at Baylor University, spring 2013, p. 18, accessed February 14, 2016, http://www.baylor.edu/content/services/document.php/193181.pdf.

2. Ibid., 18–19.

3. Aaron Milavec, *The Didache: Faith, Hope, and Life of the Earliest Christian Community, 50–70 C.E.* (New York: The Newman Press, 2003), 29.

4. Ted Olsen, "The Beginning of Lent," *Christian History* (2008), accessed February 14, 2016, http://www.christianitytoday.com/history/2008/august/beginning-of-lent.html.

5. Trinity United Church of Christ, "Fasting for the Lenten Season," March 29, 2015, accessed February 14, 2016, https://trinitychicago.org/wpcontent/uploads/2015/03/Bulletin32915readers_web.pdf.

6. Ibid.

7. Howard-John Wesley, "A Baptist View on the Imposition of Ashes," January 27, 2016, Alfred Street Baptist Church, accessed February 14, 2016, http://www.alfredstreet.org/media-and-print/a-baptist-view-on-the-imposition-of-ashes/.

8. Ibid.

CHAPTER 1

The First Week

Prayer

*Jesus, full of the Holy Spirit, returned from the Jordan and was
led by the Spirit in the wilderness.* (Luke 4:1)

There is no cure that does not cost.
—proverb, Kenya

Prayer. That's the first step toward a deep faith. It's both the preparation and the provocation that drives the Christian.

Prior to beginning his life mission, Jesus is led by the Holy Spirit
into the wilderness for a time of testing and preparation. Inasmuch
as the Holy Spirit is leading and Jesus is following, this episode suggests that Jesus is engaged in holy communication. In fact, the
Gospel of Luke ensures that we understand Jesus as a man of prayer.

Jesus heals a man covered with a skin disease, and subsequently,
his popularity is off the charts. People are drawn to him. "But he
would withdraw to deserted places and pray" (Luke 5:16). Prayer
is the first item on Jesus' agenda when he readies himself to select
his twelve apostles. "Now during the days he went out to the
mountain to pray; and he spent the night in prayer to God" (Luke
6:12). After a long day of ministering to enthusiastic crowds, and
then recognizing economic disparities were such that the neighborhood didn't have a market that could provide healthy and nutri-
tious food, Jesus cooks up a miracle meal with five loaves of bread

1

and two fish. But before giving the food to his disciples to give to the crowd, Jesus "looked up to heaven, and blessed" the food (Luke 9:16).

Luke records the Transfiguration scene in which Jesus takes Peter, John, and James with him for a mountaintop prayer meeting. "And while he was praying, the appearance of his face changed, and his clothes became dazzling white" (Luke 9:29). And after the disciples request a lesson on prayer (Luke 11:2-4), Jesus tells them:

> "When you pray, say:
>
> Father, hallowed be your name.
> Your kingdom come.
>> Give us each day our daily bread.
>> And forgive us our sins,
> for we ourselves forgive everyone indebted to us.
>> And do not bring us to the time of trial."

When Jesus is on the Mount of Olives and prays in the garden, "he prayed more earnestly, and his sweat became like great drops of blood falling down to the ground" (Luke 22:44). Jesus charges his followers to "be alert at all time, praying that you may have strength" (Luke 21:36).

Prayer is an inescapable spiritual discipline that Jesus demonstrates. As a discipline, prayer is about drawing closer to God. It's about relationship, and not a manipulative device to get what we want. As Dr. Jeremiah Wright says, "Sometimes the request is denied, and sometimes the request is delayed, but the prayer is answered. All prayer is answered."[1]

Thus, prayer is both preparatory and primary for this Lenten spiritual pilgrimage. We frame this week, and even the days to come, with and through prayer. "Open my eyes that I may see . . ."[2]

Day 1
Ash Wednesday
Rejection

When the days drew near for him to be taken up, he set his face to go to Jerusalem. And he sent messengers ahead of him. On their way they entered a village of the Samaritans to make ready for him; but they did not receive him, because his face was set toward Jerusalem. When his disciples James and John saw it, they said, "Lord, do you want us to command fire to come down from heaven and consume them?" But he turned and rebuked them. Then they went on to another village. (Luke 9:51-56)

He who is being carried does not realize how far the town is.—proverb, Nigeria

Reverend Miles Jerome Jones used to tell his students at the Samuel DeWitt Proctor School of Theology at Virginia Union University, "The call to follow Jesus is always more than an invitation to come behind him." The call to follow Jesus Christ is an invitation to grasp his lifework. And so, today we begin this season of spiritual renewal with the full knowledge that, in the Scriptures, Jesus is pushing his way to Jerusalem, where he will fulfill his purpose. Regardless of the unwarranted rejection he may have felt, his response was peaceful persistence. He continues on his way. How did you respond the last time someone mistreated you simply because of who you are, or because of the goals or dreams you have?

The massacre of nine innocent persons gathered together for Bible study at Emanuel African Methodist Episcopal Church in Charleston, South Carolina, on the evening of June 17, 2015, illustrated again the ignominious actions of racism. And the responses from many of the victims' family members demonstrated, again, how love and forgiveness overcome hatred.

On this Ash Wednesday, how do you respond to unwarranted treatment?

Prayer Focus

Have mercy on me, O God,
    according to your steadfast love;
according to your abundant mercy
    blot out my transgressions.
Wash me thoroughly from my iniquity,
    and cleanse me from my sin. . . .
Create in me a clean heart, O God,
    and put a new and right spirit within me.
—Psalm 51:1-2,10

Day 2
Thursday
Commitment

As they were going along the road, someone said to him, "I will follow you wherever you go." And Jesus said to him, "Foxes have holes, and birds of the air have nests; but the Son of Man has nowhere to lay his head." To another he said, "Follow me." But he said, "Lord, first let me go and bury my father." But Jesus said to him, "Let the dead bury their own dead; but, as for you, go and proclaim the kingdom of God." Another said, "I will follow you, Lord; but let me first say farewell to those at my home." Jesus said to him, "No one who puts a hand to the plow and looks back is fit for the kingdom of God." (Luke 9:57-62)

Leave a log in the water as long as you like: it will never be a crocodile. —proverb, Guinea-Bissau

I pledged Alpha Phi Alpha fraternity during my junior year at what is now Rowan University. Alpha is the nation's first black Greek-letter organization, started at Cornell University in 1906. During the "old school" pledging process, Big Brother William H. Myers taught us that "Excuses are the tools of the incompetent that build monuments of nothingness." His point was that excuses were unprofitable for young African American men seeking to join an organization whose objectives are

> to stimulate the ambition of its members; to prepare them for the greatest usefulness in the causes of humanity, freedom, and dignity of the individual; to encourage the highest and noblest form of manhood; and to aid downtrodden humanity in its efforts to achieve higher social, economic, and intellectual status.[3]

Excuses were not an option.

The call to follow Jesus is no less resolute. *The Message* says it this way: "No procrastination. No backward looks. You can't put God's kingdom off till tomorrow. Seize the day" (Luke 9:62). Are you putting off anything that the Lord is inviting you to do? This is a time to deny oneself and follow the Lord.

Prayer Focus

> You who live in the shelter of the Most High,
>   who abide in the shadow of the Almighty,
> will say to the LORD, "My refuge and my fortress;
>   my God, in whom I trust."
> —Psalm 91:1-2

Day 3
Friday
Mission

After this the Lord appointed seventy others and sent them on ahead of him in pairs to every town and place where he himself intended to go. He said to them, "The harvest is plentiful, but the laborers are few; therefore ask the Lord of the harvest to send out laborers into his harvest. Go on your way. See, I am sending you out like lambs into the midst of wolves. Carry no purse, no bag, no sandals; and greet no one on the road. Whatever house you enter, first say, 'Peace to this house!' And if anyone is there who shares in peace, your peace will rest on that person; but if not, it will return to you. Remain in the same house, eating and drinking whatever they provide, for the laborer deserves to be paid. Do not move about from house to house. Whenever you enter a town and its people welcome you, eat what is set before you; cure the sick who are there, and say to them, 'The kingdom of God has come near to you.'" (Luke 10:1-9)

A fool and water will go the way they are diverted.
—saying, Ethiopia

Jesus tells his disciples to remain steadfast and focused, not to get distracted, delayed, or detoured along the pilgrimage. We must refrain from the distractions along life's journey.

A young man from Rwanda was being forced by his tribe to renounce Christ or face death. He refused to renounce Christ, and his captors murdered him. The brave believer is said to have written what has come to be widely known as "The Fellowship of the Unashamed." It reads, in part:

The decision has been made. I am a disciple of Jesus Christ. I won't look back, let up, slow down, back away, or be still.

My past is redeemed, my present makes sense, and my future is secure. I am finished and done with low living, sight walking, smooth knees, colorless dreams, tamed vision, worldly talking, cheap giving, and dwarfed goals . . .

My face is set, my gait is fast, my goal is heaven, my road is narrow, my way is rough, my companions are few, my guide is reliable, my mission is clear . . . [4]

He concluded by declaring he's part of the "Fellowship of the Unashamed." In other words, he's not ashamed of the gospel of Jesus Christ, and he will remain firm in his faith. Can you make the same declaration?

Prayer Focus
> Because you have made the LORD your refuge,
>   the Most High your dwelling place,
> no evil shall befall you,
> no scourge come near your tent....
>
> Those who love me, I will deliver;
> I will protect those who know my name.
> When they call to me, I will answer them;
> I will be with them in trouble,
> I will rescue them and honor them.
> With long life I will satisfy them,
> and show them my salvation.
> —Psalm 91:9-10,14-16

Day 4
Saturday
Change

"Woe to you, Chorazin! Woe to you, Bethsaida! For if the deeds of power done in you had been done in Tyre and Sidon, they would have repented long ago, sitting in sackcloth and ashes. But at the judgement it will be more tolerable for Tyre and Sidon than for you. And you, Capernaum,
will you be exalted to heaven?
No, you will be brought down to Hades.
"Whoever listens to you listens to me, and whoever rejects you rejects me, and whoever rejects me rejects the one who sent me." (Luke 10:13-16 NRSV)

No matter how full the river, it still wants to grow.
— proverb, Congo

There are some pressure-cooker situations in our lives that ought to force immediate change. And yet, they don't. We can remain comfortable in our condition and not recognize we have a problem. Like the man at the pool in Bethsaida (John 5:1-17), we remain far too long in a bad situation. We're reluctant to change.

Some years ago, while serving as pastor at historic Gillfield Baptist Church (Petersburg, VA), the congregational leaders wanted to vote on whether we would permit drums in worship. "Why do we have to vote on drums?" I asked, adding, "We've never voted on whether to allow the use of a harp or violin in worship." Including drums in worship was change, and change can be emotional.

So often when we talk about taking risks and bold change, we borrow that corporate mantra: "If you always do what you've always done, you will always get what you've always had." The lesson is that you can't continue doing the same thing and expect to get different results. Bishop Kenneth Ulmer, senior pastor at the thirteen-thousand-member megachurch Faithful Central Bible Church in Inglewood, California, has often said, "Healthy things grow. Growing requires change. Change challenges us. Challenge forces us to trust God. Trust leads to obedience. Obedience makes us healthy. Healthy things grow!" But do we really believe it? Jesus asked the man at the pool, "Do you want to be made whole?" Do you really?

Let this be a season of repentance.

Prayer Focus

For everything there is a season, and a time for every matter
under heaven:
a time to be born, and a time to die;
a time to plant, and a time to pluck up what is planted;
a time to kill, and a time to heal;
a time to break down, and a time to build up;
a time to weep, and a time to laugh;
a time to mourn, and a time to dance;
. . . a time to tear, and a time to sew;
a time to keep silence, and a time to speak;
a time to love, and a time to hate;
a time for war, and a time for peace.
—Ecclesiastes 3:1-4,7-8

Day 5
First Sunday in Lent[5]
Purpose

The seventy returned with joy, saying, "Lord, in your name even the demons submit to us!" He said to them, "I watched Satan fall from heaven like a flash of lightning. See, I have given you authority to tread on snakes and scorpions, and over all the power of the enemy; and nothing will hurt you.

Nevertheless, do not rejoice at this, that the spirits submit to you, but rejoice that your names are written in heaven." (Luke 10:17-20)

To the person who seizes two things, one slips from his grasp!—proverb, Swahili

I served as a regional minister for American Baptist Churches of New Jersey. It was a great joy to work with about 120 congregations in the Essex and North New Jersey associations. In addition to African American congregations, I also served African, Anglo, Asian, Haitian, Hispanic, and Portuguese churches.

One disturbing aspect of the job was witnessing a church's decline. Local churches experience life cycles and can die. As Thom Rainer points out in *Autopsy of a Deceased Church*, "As the church lost her purpose, she slowly but surely began to die. . . . A church without a gospel-centered purpose is no longer a church at all."[6] In his book, Rainer conducts "autopsies" on fourteen churches. The intent is to determine "cause of death." Invariably, the deceased churches stopped "being" the church long before their demise. In other words, they forgot their purpose for being.

Jesus admonishes his followers to stay sober and focused on the purpose: celebrate salvation, not domination. They are not to become "enamored of the sensational." *The Baker Illustrated Bible Commentary* points out, "The crucial thing is not the explosion of demons and powers over evil but the assurance of having one's name written in God's book."[7]

This first week of Lent, which began on Ash Wednesday and ends today, concludes with a reminder that Christians remain faithful to their salvific lifestyle.

Prayer Focus

> The LORD is my rock, my fortress, and my deliverer,
> my God, my rock, in whom I take refuge,
> my shield and the horn of my salvation,
> my stronghold and my refuge,
> my savior; you save me from violence.
> I call upon the LORD, who is worthy to be praised,
> and I am saved from my enemies.
> —2 Samuel 22:2-4

Group Discussion on Prayer

1. What is Lent? What is its significance in the life of the church?
2. Which spiritual disciplines are given special consideration during the Lenten season?
3. Why is it necessary to begin the Lenten devotional journey with prayer?
4. Describe your present prayer life. What does a powerful prayer life look like?
5. In what ways have you experienced the pain of rejection? Discuss the way in which you responded in the past, and how you can respond in the future.
6. Discuss your congregation's vision, its effectiveness in advancing the vision, and the role of spirituality in fulfilling the vision.

Personal Action

1. Schedule time to pray—every day . . . and then do it!
2. Develop a prayer journal. Write down and meditate upon the ways in which you discern God's movement in response to your prayers. What are the varied ways in which you have witnessed God respond to your prayers in the past?
3. As an expression of the love of Christ, pray for your enemies.
4. The Bible tells us in Psalm 37:5: "Commit your way to the

L ORD; trust in him, and he will act." Start your daily devotions by presenting to God your plans for the day. Instead of a "to-do" list, you're developing a "to-God" list; you're taking it out of your hands and placing it in God's hands.

5. Develop a seven-day prayer calendar for next week, with a special focus for each day of the week.

6. What does the Bible say about prayer? Here are some Scriptures you can study: Deuteronomy 4:29; Psalm 17:1; Psalm 25:1; Psalm 145:18; Jeremiah 25:13; Matthew 6:6; Matthew 14:23; 1 Timothy 2:8; Hebrews 4:16; Hebrews 10:22.

Notes

1. Jeremiah Wright, in J. Alfred Smith Sr., *No Other Help I Know: Sermons on Prayer and Spirituality* (Valley Forge, PA: Judson Press, 1996), 90.

2. Clara H. Scott, "Open My Eyes, That I May See," *The New National Baptist Hymnal* (Nashville: Triad Publications, 2001), #218.

3. Alpha Phi Alpha Fraternity, Inc., "Our Mission," last modified September 3, 2015, accessed February 13, 2016, http://www.apa1906.net.

4. Dr. Bob Moorhead, "Rwandan Man's Confession," The Way of the Master television, accessed September 13, 2016, http://www.wayofthemaster.com/confes sion.shtml.

5. Week 1 of Lent begins on Ash Wednesday; therefore, the week has only five devotions.

6. Thom S. Rainer, *Autopsy of a Deceased Church: 12 Ways to Keep Yours Alive* (Nashville: B&H Books, 2014), 75.

7. Thomas R. Schreiner, "Luke," in *The Baker Illustrated Bible Commentary*, ed. Gary M. Burge and Andrew E. Hill (Grand Rapids, MI: Baker Books, 2012), 1082.

CHAPTER 2

The Second Week

Fasting

*Jesus, full of the Holy Spirit, returned from the Jordan and
was led by the Spirit in the wilderness, where for forty days he
was tempted by the devil. He ate nothing at all during those days,
and when they were over, he was famished.* (Luke 4:1-2)

Something on the inside, working on the outside;
I feel a change in my life.
—Wyatt Tee Walker, *Spirits That Dwell in Deep Woods*

Dr. William Marcus Small (New Calvary Baptist Church, Norfolk,
VA) and his wife, Cassandra, held an Afrocentric rite of passage
into adulthood ceremony for their son—my godson—Malcolm.
The African ritual commemorates a male's transition from boy-
hood into manhood. Rites of passage are important celebrations
because they acknowledge significant milestones in life, such as
birth, puberty, marriage, and death. For Malcolm, the ceremony
marked his sixteenth birthday.

Jesus is participating in a rite of passage as he takes his journey
into the wilderness for forty days of spiritual reflection and testing.
He will never be the same. He emerges from the wilderness spiritually strengthened and prepared to accept his life mission. His
quest in the wilderness includes fasting.

This week we consider that when it comes to spiritual devotion, there is prayer without fasting, but not fasting without prayer.

The Lenten season requires "giving up" and "letting go" of something in order to redeem it or replace it with that which is far more enriching, edifying, and inspirational. Typically, we shift our focus from food to faith. We give up McDonald's burgers and Dunkin' Donuts coffee. And as Minister Johnie Hopkins pointed out one night in our Bible study, without spirituality as its starting point, fasting can merely become a weight-loss program. It becomes a cleansing of the body, which, by itself, does have health benefits.

Spiritual fasting requires the decision to "turn down the plate" and put aside some activities that are then replaced with prayer and spiritual contemplation. The *Tyndale Bible Dictionary* points out: "Three types of fast are generally recognized: *normal*, in which there is no intake for a prescribed period of time, though there may be an intake of liquids; *partial*, in which the diet is limited, though some food is allowed; and *absolute*, in which there is a total abstinence from food and liquids in all forms."[1]

The early Christian handbook *Didache* (circa 50 CE), gives no real detailed instruction on fasting, but it does link fasting with baptism, as if to suggest that fasting intensifies the conversion. New Testament scholar Dr. Aaron Milavec suggests: "Fasting and prayer might help one come to grips with all the hopes and dreams that conversion to a new way of life demanded. Fasting, therefore, had the effect of intensifying an already existing state of being clearminded, focused, urgent."[2]

The Bible is replete with examples of persons and communities fasting. For example, Israel fasted: "You shall eat no bread or parched grain or fresh ears until the very day, until you have brought the offering of your God: It is a statute forever throughout your generations in all your settlements" (Leviticus 23:14).

David fasted when he was spiritually distressed: "Then Nathan went to his house. The LORD struck the child that Uriah's wife bore to David, and it became very ill. David therefore pleaded with God for the child; David fasted and went in and lay all night on the ground. The elders of his house stood beside him, urging him to get up from the ground, but he would not, nor did he eat food with them" (2 Samuel 12:15-17).

Anna the prophetess fasted: "There was also a prophet, Anna the daughter of Phanuel, of the tribe of Asher. She was of a great age, having lived with her husband seven years after her marriage, then as a widow until the age of eighty-four. She never left the temple but worshiped there with fasting and prayer night and day" (Luke 2:36-37).

There is an episode recorded in Mark's Gospel (9:14-32) when Jesus heals a demon-possessed boy. The boy's father had brought him to Jesus' disciples in order to be healed, but they cannot successfully perform the exorcism. Jesus, however, speaks boldly to the demon: "You spirit that keeps this boy from speaking and hearing, I command you, come out of him, and never enter him again!" The demonic departs quickly. Later, in private, the disciples inquire as to why they could not do what Jesus did. The Lord replied, "This kind can come out only through prayer." The Revised Standard Version includes the annotation: "Other ancient authorities add *and fasting.*"

Fasting is accompanied with humility and prayer. It's an act of worship that requires a repentant heart. In Jesus' Parable of the Pharisee and the Tax Collector (Luke 18:9-14), the socially downcast tax collector "went home justified before God" because of his humble heart.

Fast this week, allowing God to respond to your spiritual emptiness. Let God fill you with the spiritual sustenance to demonstrate forgiveness, engage in reconciliation, and walk in holiness. Use this as a time of reflection, release, and restoration.

Day 6
Monday
Devotion

At that same hour Jesus rejoiced in the Holy Spirit and said, "I thank you, Father, Lord of heaven and earth, because you have hidden these things from the wise and the intelligent and have revealed them to infants; yes, Father, for such was your gracious will. All things have been handed over to me by my Father; and no one knows who the Son is except the Father, or who the Father is except the Son and anyone to whom the Son chooses to reveal him."

Then turning to the disciples, Jesus said to them privately, "Blessed are the eyes that see what you see! For I tell you that many prophets and kings desired to see what you see, but did not see it, and to hear what you hear, but did not hear it." (Luke 10:21-24)

It's a black thing—you wouldn't understand.—saying

Jesus has tremendous love and regard for children. When his disciples determined that he was too busy to bless some children that mothers had brought to him, he corrected them by saying, "Let the little children come to me, and do not stop them; for it is to such as these that the kingdom of heaven belongs" (Matthew 19:14). And on another occasion, he said, "If any of you put a stumbling block before one of these little ones who believe in me, it would be better for you if a great millstone were fastened around your neck and you were drowned in the depth of the sea" (Matthew 18:6).

Open and broad-minded innocence, such as a child possesses, makes one ready to receive what Jesus has to offer. The Lord desires our full devotion, both head and heart. It takes more than wisdom and intelligence to see, hear, and do the ways of God.

Prayer Focus
> I call upon you, for you will answer me, O God;
> incline your ear to me, hear my words.
> —Psalm 17:6

Day 7
Tuesday
Do Likewise

But wanting to justify himself, he asked Jesus, "And who is my neighbor?" Jesus replied, "A man was going down from Jerusalem to Jericho, and fell into the hands of robbers, who stripped him, beat him, and went away, leaving him half dead. Now by chance a priest was going down that road; and when he saw him, he passed by on the other side. So likewise a Levite, when he came to the place and saw him, passed by on the other side. But a Samaritan while traveling came near him; and when he saw him, he was moved with pity. He went to him and bandaged his wounds, having poured oil and wine on them. Then he put him on his own animal, brought him to an inn, and took care of him. The next day he took out two denarii, gave them to the innkeeper, and said, 'Take care of him; and when I come back, I will repay you whatever more you spend.' Which of these three, do you think, was a neighbor to the man who fell into the hands of the robbers?" He said, "The one who showed him mercy." Jesus said to him, "Go and do likewise." (Luke 10:29-37)

Each one teach one.—Reconstruction era motto

On a cold winter night, November 14, 2012, New York City police officer Lawrence DePrimo, twenty-five, was working the counterterrorism beat near Times Square. He heard laughter, and noticed someone was laughing at a homeless man who had neither socks nor shoes. His blistered feet could be seen from a distance. The officer asked the man if he had anything to cover his feet. "It's okay, sir, I've never had a pair of shoes," the homeless man replied. "But God bless you."[3] At that moment, the young officer considered that his job was to protect and serve. And at that moment, the greatest need for the homeless man was a pair of shoes.

The police officer walked to a nearby shoe store on West 42nd Street and, with his own money, bought a pair of waterproof winter boots. The homeless man's face lit up when DePrimo gave him the boots. Using a cellphone, a tourist snapped a picture of the police officer, on one knee, giving the boots to the barefoot homeless man. She sent the picture to NYPD. The department posted the image on its Facebook page. The post immediately went viral. Officer DePrimo became an Internet hero because of the kinship he felt for this homeless man. When interviewed by *NBC News* correspondent Stephanie Gosk, the police officer said he just did "what anybody would do."[4] Jesus says, "Go and do likewise."

Prayer Focus

Let the favor of the LORD our God be upon us,
and prosper for us the work of our hands—
O prosper the work of our hands!
—Psalm 90:17

Day 8
Wednesday
Distractions

Now as they went on their way, he entered a certain village, where a woman named Martha welcomed him into her home. She had a sister named Mary, who sat at the Lord's feet and listened to what he was saying. But Martha was distracted by her many tasks; so she came to him and asked, "Lord, do you not care that my sister has left me to do all the work by myself? Tell her then to help me." But the Lord answered her, "Martha, Martha, you are worried and distracted by many things; there is need of only one thing. Mary has chosen the better part, which will not be taken away from her." (Luke 10:38-42)

One cannot count on riches.—Proverb from Somalia

In his book *Preaching to the Black Middle Class*, Marvin McMickle writes about his concern that we can become so busy making money, attending social events, and being involved in clubs and boards and organizations that we have no time for God and family. He argues that "there is the danger that as our economic prosperity increases, our relationship with God and God's people may be allowed to decrease. We may become so caught up with our clubs, fraternal groups, cotillions, cabarets, and cocktail parties, that we allow a serious relationship with God to become only a marginal aspect of our lives."[5]

The "abundant life" is found in spending time with the Lord. During this season, change your diet in more ways than the food you abstain from consuming. Demonstrate self-restraint also in your social aspirations and in your materialistic consumption. Leave it up to Jesus Christ to fill any void that creates a hunger in your spirit.

Prayer Focus

> One thing I asked of the LORD,
> that will I seek after:
> to live in the house of the LORD
> all the days of my life,

to behold the beauty of the LORD,
and to inquire in his temple.
—Psalm 27:4

Day 9
Thursday
Hypocrisy

Meanwhile, when the crowd gathered in thousands, so that they trampled on one another, he began to speak first to his disciples, "Beware of the yeast of the Pharisees, that is, their hypocrisy. Nothing is covered up that will not be uncovered, and nothing secret that will not become known. Therefore whatever you have said in the dark will be heard in the light, and what you have whispered behind closed doors will be proclaimed from the housetops." (Luke 12:1-3)

When spiderwebs unite, they can tie up a lion.
—proverb, Ethiopia

The Reverend Dr. Martin Luther King Jr. addressed America's hypocrisy when he stood before a tremendous crowd of more than 250,000 at the Lincoln Memorial on August 28, 1963, and shared the "I Have a Dream" speech. He began by saying:

Five score years ago, a great American, in whose symbolic shadow we stand signed the Emancipation Proclamation. This momentous decree came as a great beacon light of hope to millions of Negro slaves who had been seared in the flames of withering injustice. It came as a joyous daybreak to end the long night of captivity. . . .

But one hundred years later, we must face the tragic fact that the Negro is still not free. One hundred years later, the life of the Negro is still sadly crippled by the manacles of segregation and the chains of discrimination. One hundred years later, the Negro lives on a lonely island of poverty in the midst of a vast ocean of material prosperity. One hundred years later, the Negro is still languishing in the corners of American society and finds himself an exile in his own land. So we have come here today to dramatize an appalling condition.[6]

And while Dr. King shed light on our country's despicable condition, he also challenged our nation to truly be united. Community is really about *unity* and *harmony*.

Prayer Focus
For I am convinced that neither death, nor life, nor angels, nor rulers, nor things present, nor things to come, nor powers, nor height, nor depth, nor anything else in all creation, will be able to separate us from the love of God in Christ Jesus our Lord.
—Romans 8:38-39

Day 10
Friday
Confession

"I tell you, my friends, do not fear those who kill the body, and after that can do nothing more. But I will warn you whom to fear: fear him who, after he has killed, has authority to cast into hell. Yes, I tell you, fear him! Are not five sparrows sold for two pennies? Yet not one of them is forgotten in God's sight. But even the hairs of your head are all counted. Do not be afraid; you are of more value than many sparrows.

"And I tell you, everyone who acknowledges me before others, the Son of Man also will acknowledge before the angels of God; but whoever denies me before others will be denied before the angels of God." (Luke 12:4-9)

If you can't bear no cross, you can't wear no crown.
—saying

True Christian conversion means a readiness for suffering and ill treatment. Jesus conveys this truth by drawing a comparison with the noisy and energetic little sparrow. The bird was well known in ancient Greece and Egypt; it's common in the Holy Land. God's remembrance of the little sparrow does not prevent it from being sold as an object of sacrifice. Likewise, God's care and concern for us does not preempt us from suffering affliction, anguish, and abuse. But because of God's grace, we stand and respond differently.

There's a story among preachers about a talking teacup.[7] A lady traveled to England, and while she was there, purchased a beautiful teacup. On her voyage home, the woman fell asleep and dreamed that her teacup could talk.

The cup said, "I know you admire the way I look now, but I did not always look this way." The teacup then recounted its story of being shapeless and without form. It told how it was forcefully molded, and beat down, and molded some more. It spoke about being placed in a hot kiln, an oven even hotter than you can imagine. The cup went on to explain, "I learned to thank that master craftsman because if he had not molded me, I'd be shapeless and without form. If he had not put me in the oven of oppression, I'd have no structural integrity. If he had not put paint on me, I'd have no color. If he had not put me back in the oven to bake me again, I would fall apart."

The apostle Paul said, "We also boast of our troubles, because we know that trouble produces endurance, endurance brings

God's approval, and his approval creates hope. This hope does not disappoint us, for God has poured out his love into our hearts by means of the Holy Spirit, who is God's gift to us" (Romans 5:3-5, GNT).

Prayer Focus

> For now we see in a mirror, dimly, but then we will see face to face. Now I know only in part; then I will know fully, even as I have been fully known. —1 Corinthians 13:12

Day 11
Saturday
Worry

He said to his disciples, "Therefore I tell you, do not worry about your life, what you will eat, or about your body, what you will wear. For life is more than food, and the body more than clothing. Consider the ravens: they neither sow nor reap, they have neither storehouse nor barn, and yet God feeds them. Of how much more value are you than the birds! And can any of you by worrying add a single hour to your span of life?" (Luke 12:22-25)

I know one thing we did right
Was the day we started to fight,
Keep your eyes on the prize,
Hold on.
—civil rights era song

Reflect on the priorities in your life. Give thoughtful consideration to what is really important. As Jesus is moving toward Jerusalem with his disciples, he reminds them not to worry about temporal things. Frugality is a virtue.

We live in a microwave era. Folks thrive on instant gratification. However, Jesus is saying that we can refrain from some things. He is not suggesting that we disregard, ignore, or overlook those things we need. But Jesus is saying that in spite of how discouraging or disparaging or disheartening the condition of our existence may appear to be—God can handle it! There is no use fretting over it. All of life is simply not an emergency.

Don't feel anxious about your life. No use walking around all tense and uptight, all wound up like a clock, feeling perilous about your predicament. The birds of the air neither plant nor gather, and God takes care of them. Consider the lilies of the field; they are here today and gone tomorrow, and yet God takes care of them.

Be concerned and prepared and make provisions, but don't worry about how you're going to make it! Whatever you need, God has it! Worry produces fear. Worry robs you of your faith. Worrying is an obstacle. Jesus says to each of us, "And can any of you by worrying add a single hour to your span of life?"

The God who created you can be trusted to take care of you.

Prayer Focus
> You are my God, and I will give thanks to you;
> you are my God, I will extol you.
>
> O give thanks to the LORD, for he is good,
> for his steadfast love endures forever.
> —Psalm 118:28-29

Day 12
Second Sunday in Lent
Relevancy

On one occasion when Jesus was going to the house of a leader of the Pharisees to eat a meal on the sabbath, they were watching him closely. Just then, in front of him, there was a man who had dropsy. And Jesus asked the lawyers and Pharisees, "Is it lawful to cure people on the sabbath, or not?" But they were silent. So Jesus took him and healed him, and sent him away. Then he said to them, "If one of you has a child or an ox that has fallen into a well, will you not immediately pull it out on a sabbath day?" And they could not reply to this. (Luke 14:1-6)

When you pray for rain, you've got to deal with the mud, too.—Caribbean saying

The religious leaders in Jesus' day said that it was unlawful to heal on the Sabbath. The Sabbath was supposed to be a day when all work ceased. The day that was set aside for rest, but the spirit of honoring God became lost in a labyrinth of laws. The rigorous rules and regulations were so exhaustive that, as the *Tyndale Bible Dictionary* points out, "the main purpose of the Sabbath became lost beneath a mass of legalistic detail."[8] As Jesus said in Mark 2:27, "The sabbath was made for humankind, and not humankind for the sabbath."

There is a line from the old movie *Green Pastures* in which Noah says to God, "People around here don't do much church-going. They mostly use Sunday to get over what they did all night on Saturday." It is probably safe to say that recovering from a hangover (or other natural consequences from a Saturday night of excess) is not what God intended in establishing the Sabbath as a

25

day of rest and re-creation!

The local church faces many challenges in this age. One of most prominent challenges for the modern church is to remain relevant. This is often a Herculean task for older, established historic congregations. In *Unfinished Evangelism*, author Tim Wright argues that tradition can turn into traditionalism. This is when "tradition becomes an anchor holding the church to the post rather than a rudder guiding it into the future."[9]

The church must break some chains and tear down some idols in order to stay true to the spirit and authentic intent of the gospel.

Prayer Focus

The LORD is near to all who call on him,
to all who call on him in truth.
He fulfills the desire of all who fear him;
he also hears their cry, and saves them.
The LORD watches over all who love him,
but all the wicked he will destroy.
—Psalm 145:18-20

Group Discussion on Fasting

1. Discuss your progress toward spiritual growth and renewal. Has God spoken to you this past week? In what way? What was the message? What was your response?
2. What is spiritual fasting? Discuss the differences between normal, partial, and absolute fasts.
3. Should a person with health concerns participate in an absolute fast? If not, why?
4. In what way was Jesus "full" after a period of fasting in the wilderness?
5. Examine the ways in which your church is intentionally receiving and discipling children and youth.
6. What distractions are hindering you from spending more

time with God? What are you willing to do about it?
7. How do you handle the problems in your life? Discuss biblical responses to life's problems.

Personal Action
1. Refrain from eating your favorite food, and replace it with an insatiable appetite for reading the Bible and meditating on God's goodness.
2. Give up social media (for a while). Given the fact that the United States is so technologically connected and operating on information overload, determine a time to fast from using the various social media platforms.
3. As a Bible study group, commit to a season of fasting. Encourage the group members to share their prayer concerns, and have someone write them down. Distribute the list to the group members so that everyone can take the group concerns before the Lord in prayer. Set a date to offer prayer and praise reports.

Notes
1. Walter A. Elwell and Philip W. Comfort, "Fast, Fasting," *Tyndale Bible Dictionary* (Wheaton, IL: Tyndale House, 2001), 478.
2. Aaron Milavec, *The Didache: Faith, Hope, and Life of the Earliest Christian Communities, 50–70 C.E.* (New York: The Newman Press, 2003), 253.
3. Amanda Mikelberg and Joe Kemp, "NYPD Officer Larry DePrimo Immortalized in Tourist's Photo after Giving Barefoot Homeless Man a Pair of Boots," *New York Daily News*, updated December 18, 2012, accessed February 13, 2016, http://www.nydailynews.com/new-york/generosity-immortalized-photo-article-1.1210565.
4. Stephanie Gosk, "After Officer's Gift, Homeless Man 'Lit up Like It Was Christmas,'" *NBC Nightly News*, November 29, 2012, accessed September 14, 2016, http://www.nbcnews.com/video/nightly-news/50018787.
5. Marvin McMickle, *Preaching to the Black Middle Class: Words of Challenge, Words of Hope* (Valley Forge, PA: Judson Press, 2000), 98.
6. James M. Washington, *I Have a Dream: Writings and Speeches That Changed the World* (San Francisco: HarperSanFrancisco, 1992), 102.
7. H. Beecher Hicks, *Preaching Through a Storm* (Grand Rapids, MI: Ministry

Resources Library, 1987), 109.

    8. Elwell and Comfort, "Sabbath," *Tyndale Bible Dictionary*, 1148.

    9. Tim Wright, *Unfinished Evangelism: More Than Getting Them in the Door* (Minneapolis: Augsburg Fortress, 1995), 36.

CHAPTER 3

The Third Week

Almsgiving

Then Jesus, filled with the power of the Spirit,
returned to Galilee. (Luke 4:14)

If you only give half of yourself, you only become
half of who you're supposed to be.
—Jeff Johnson, *Everything I'm Not Made Me*
Everything I Am

Our church's benevolence ministry provides emergency finances to individuals and families in crisis. The Helping Hands Ministry provides meals on Tuesdays to the neighborhood's homeless community or those too financially strapped to afford a meal; volunteers serve about six thousand meals a year. We also operate a food pantry that provides meats, vegetables, and canned goods to the needy. All of this work of the church is missions, and an expression of what has traditionally been called almsgiving. Alms are kind deeds as an expression of compassion and mercy. Generally, we think of food and money. The first deacons' primary function in Acts 6 was to distribute alms.

Almsgiving is the focus this third week of Lent. When we give alms, we're giving to the needy without any expectation of anything in return. We can widen the scope of this spiritual discipline and see almsgiving as a holistic practice. It's theological, spiritual, and mission-minded. It's wholeheartedly helping and giving of one's heart to improve the conditions of the poor and those in need. It becomes a head, heart, and hands approach.

Theologian Henri J. M. Nouwen (1932–1996) wrote in his seminal work, *The Wounded Healer*:

> How does our Liberator come? I found an old legend in the Talmud which may suggest to us the beginning of an answer:
>
> Rabbi Yoshua ben Levi came upon Elijah the prophet while he was standing at the entrance of Rabbi Simeron ben Yohai's cave . . . he asked Elijah, "When will the Messiah come?" Elijah replied, "Go and ask him yourself."
>
> "Where is he?"
>
> "Sitting at the gates of the city."
>
> "How shall I know him?"
>
> "He is sitting among the poor covered with wounds. The others unbind all their wounds at the same time and then bind them up again. But he unbinds one at a time and binds it up again, saying to himself, 'Perhaps I shall be needed: if so I must always be ready so as not to delay for a moment.'" (Taken from the Sanhedrin)
>
> The Messiah, the story tells us, is sitting among the poor, binding his wounds one at a time, waiting for the moment when he is needed.[1]

Following the wilderness experience, Jesus returned to Galilee where he is needed. He returns to wholeheartedly and sacrificially give of himself. He returns with the fire and focus, the Holy Ghost spirit and mission-mindedness to redeem the world and transform conditions for the abandoned, exploited, powerless, and burdened.

Consider the following:

1. Black infants are nearly two-and-one half times more likely than white infants to die before their first birthday.[2]
2. More than 2.2 million African Americans have diabetes.[3]
3. Black women are diagnosed with AIDS at a rate twenty-five times that of white women.[4]
4. One of every three black males born today can expect to go to prison in his lifetime.[5]
5. Across the United States, more than 10 percent of black drivers stopped by police were likely to be searched or have their vehicle searched, as opposed to 3.5 percent of white drivers stopped by police.[6]
6. The unemployment rate for black people nationwide is twice that for whites.[7]
7. African Americans have a median net worth of $5,998, compared with $88,651 for whites. Even more alarming, 32 percent of African Americans have a zero or negative net worth.[8]
8. Nearly 51 percent of African Americans have access to a home computer compared with 74.6 percent of whites. In terms of Internet access, only 40.5 percent of African Americans have access to the Internet at home compared with 67.3 percent of whites.[9]

As I was typing these words in August 2016, people in Flint, Michigan, were facing a lead poisoning crisis of epic propositions because of the political disregard for an impoverished community comprised mostly of black folk. *The Covenant with Black America—Ten Years Later* reports on this type of environmental injustice: "Lead poisoning continues to be the number-one environmental health threat to children of color in the United States, especially poor children and children living in inner cities."[10]

Almsgiving requires that we exercise authentic stewardship, with the willingness and desire to give up and let go of our valuable time, spiritual gifts, and economic resources. Be intentional in your giving this week. Let it spark a fire in you that burns beyond this holy expedition.

Day 13
Monday
Discipleship

Now large crowds were traveling with him; and he turned and said to them, "Whoever comes to me and does not hate father and mother, wife and children, brothers and sisters, yes, and even life itself, cannot be my disciple. Whoever does not carry the cross and follow me cannot be my disciple. For which of you, intending to build a tower, does not first sit down and estimate the cost, to see whether he has enough to complete it? Otherwise, when he has laid a foundation and is not able to finish, all who see it will begin to ridicule him, saying, 'This fellow began to build and was not able to finish.' Or what king, going out to wage war against another king, will not sit down first and consider whether he is able with ten thousand to oppose the one who comes against him with twenty thousand? If he cannot, then, while the other is still far away, he sends a delegation and asks for the terms of peace. So therefore, none of you can become my disciple if you do not give up all your possessions." (Luke 14:25-33)

Follow the North Star. —Underground Railroad instruction

Jesus was a master of rhetoric and literary devices. He used metaphor, saying, "I am the bread of life. Whoever comes to me will never be hungry, and whoever believes in me will never be thirsty" (John 6:35). He used paradox, saying, "Whoever wants to be first must be last of all and servant of all" (Mark 9:35). And here, as he and his disciples traveled, the master wordsmith used hyperbole to share a message about radical allegiance to the gospel.

Hyperbole is an exaggerated statement that is meant to hammer home a point. It's not to be taken literally. Therefore, Jesus was telling his followers, in no uncertain terms, that serious discipleship requires a commitment that is unwavering, unfaltering, unflinching. Have you seriously considered the cost of Christian discipleship?

The cross of forgiveness can be heavy, but are you willing to carry it?

Prayer Focus
> O give thanks to the LORD, call on his name,
> make known his deeds among the peoples.
> Sing to him, sing praises to him;
> tell of all his wonderful works.
> Glory in his holy name;
> let the hearts of those who seek the LORD rejoice.
> Seek the LORD and his strength;
> seek his presence continually.
> Remember the wonderful works he has done,
> his miracles, and the judgments he has uttered,
> O offspring of his servant Abraham,
> children of Jacob, his chosen ones.
> —Psalm 105:1-6

Day 14
Tuesday
Salt

"Salt is good; but if salt has lost its taste, how can its saltiness be restored? It is fit neither for the soil nor for the manure pile; they throw it away. Let anyone with ears to hear listen!"
(Luke 14:34-35)

I got a crown, you got a crown,
all God's chillun got a crown.
— "All God's Chillun Got Wings," Negro spiritual

Salt in the first-century Middle East was a preservative. It was used to preserve food, especially meat. Salt was also used to enhance the flavor of foods. Again, Jesus used strong rhetoric to communicate his message about the imperative nature of the Christian lifestyle to make a positive difference. It's as though Jesus was saying that a Christian disciple who does not enhance his or her community is worthless. He was calling us to be salty saints!

I learned about salty saints one day when I was shopping in Walmart. I discovered that Walmart sells a variety of salts. It sells table salt, popcorn salt, and sea salt. I also noticed it sells something called salt substitute. It's for salt-free diets. It resembles salt and tastes somewhat like salt, but it's not salt. It's salt substitute.

That's when I realized that there are times when we in the church can operate like salt substitute. And Jesus warned against this. Salt substitute has the form of faith, but it's empty. Salt substitute does just enough to appear holy: wearing the symbols, toting the Bible, quoting chapter and verse. But really . . . no more than salt substitute.

Salt substitute will always weigh public opinion before taking an unpopular position for the kingdom of God. That's salt substitute! But salty saints are living the Word, praying in faith, being in fellowship with other believers, witnessing to the world, and ministering to others. Jesus declared in no uncertain terms, "You are the salt of the earth; but if salt has lost its taste, how can it saltiness be restored? It is no longer good for anything, but is thrown out and trampled underfoot."

That's harsh language. But we need to understand that pure salt does not deteriorate. It's unheard-of for it to fall apart; it is beyond belief that it will wear away, incredible to think that it will disintegrate or decay. So, Jesus was using tough language to hammer home his point. Jesus was saying it should be as unthinkable for his disciples to lose their moral and ethical Christian character as for salt to become salt-less. It just should not happen—to the extent that if it does, Jesus says that disciple is good for nothing.

One final thought about salt: it's very ordinary. Read the record. Jesus launched his ministry with unrefined, insignificant folk. They were fearful of the pilgrimage. They sought opportunity to have some prerogatives in their lives. Some were thoughtless and others were cautious. Then and now, those who follow in the footsteps of Jesus have nothing to offer but ourselves. We're turning our ordinary lives over the Master. Jesus meets us in our ordinariness.

Years ago I worked as a news and features assistant at NBC Radio Network News. I heard that Rosa Parks was going to be a guest on the *Today Show*. (This was when Bryant Gumbel was making his own headlines because he was the first African American co-anchor of *Today*.) At just the right time, I slipped out of the radio newsroom and made my way to the *Today* studio. The timing was just right! The plan was to introduce myself to *the* Rosa Parks. This was the grandmother of the civil rights movement. She was the catalyst for the greatest movement of the twentieth century. If it had not been for Rosa Parks, there would not have been a young Baptist minister from the South—named Martin Luther King Jr.—who was catapulted into history when he shared "I Have a Dream."

But all of my preconceptions were out the window when I saw Rosa Parks. Mrs. Parks was not at all what I imagined. There was nothing magnificent or majestic about her. She was not amazing, astounding, astonishing. In fact, she was ordinary. Undistinguished. Unpretentious. She could have been anybody's auntie or madea or big momma. You could call her salt of the earth.

The Lord spoke clearly to me that day: "I use ordinary people to do extraordinary things."

Prayer Focus

"But I say to you that listen, Love your enemies, do good to those who hate you, bless those who curse you, pray for those who abuse you. If anyone strikes you on the cheek, offer the other also; and from anyone who takes away your coat do not withhold even your shirt. Give to everyone who begs from you; and if anyone takes away your goods, do not ask for them again. Do to others as you would have them do to you." —Luke 6:27-31

Day 15
Wednesday
Wealth

"There was a rich man who was dressed in purple and fine linen and who feasted sumptuously every day. And at his gate lay a poor man named Lazarus, covered with sores, who longed to satisfy his hunger with what fell from the rich man's table; even the dogs would come and lick his sores. The poor man died and was carried away by the angels to be with Abraham. The rich man also died and was buried. In Hades, where he was being tormented, he looked up and saw Abraham far away with Lazarus by his side. He called out, 'Father Abraham, have mercy on me, and send Lazarus to dip

the tip of his finger in water and cool my tongue; for I am in agony in these flames.' But Abraham said, 'Child, remember that during your lifetime you received your good things, and Lazarus in like manner evil things; but now he is comforted here, and you are in agony. Besides all this, between you and us a great chasm has been fixed, so that those who might want to pass from here to you cannot do so, and no one can cross from there to us.' He said, 'Then, father, I beg you to send him to my father's house—for I have five brothers—that he may warn them, so that they will not also come into this place of torment.' Abraham replied, 'They have Moses and the prophets; they should listen to them.' He said, 'No, father Abraham; but if someone goes to them from the dead, they will repent.' He said to him, 'If they do not listen to Moses and the prophets, neither will they be convinced even if someone rises from the dead.'" (Luke 16:19-31)

It takes a village to raise a child. — African saying

The Children's Defense Fund (CDF) reports, "The United States has the second highest child poverty rate among 35 industrialized countries despite having the largest economy in the world."[11] The CDF has unveiled a plan that shows "by investing an additional two percent of the federal budget into existing programs and policies that increase employment, make work pay, and ensure children's basic needs are met, the nation could reduce child poverty by 60 percent and lift 6.6 million children out of poverty."[12]

Founded by civil rights activist Marian Wright Edelman in 1973, the CDF has been a strong voice and unyielding advocate for children struggling to survive and thrive in impoverished conditions. In Jesus' Parable of the Rich Man and Lazarus, we are given a picture of the juxtaposition of wealth and poverty. Paul John Isaak writes in *Africa Bible Commentary*: "The topic of relationship

JOURNEY WITH JESUS THROUGH LENT

between rich and poor Christians is of importance because God is on the side of the disadvantaged and oppressed and expects his followers to stand with him."[13] It's the mission of the local church to unite, speak, and act on behalf of the powerless. Children are the most vulnerable.

Prayer Focus

> Love the LORD, all you his saints.
> The LORD preserves the faithful,
> but abundantly repays the one who acts haughtily.
> Be strong, and let your heart take courage,
> all you who wait for the LORD.
> —Psalm 31:23-24

Day 16
Thursday
Thankful

On the way to Jerusalem Jesus was going through the region between Samaria and Galilee. As he entered a village, ten lepers approached him. Keeping their distance, they called out, saying, "Jesus, Master, have mercy on us!" When he saw them, he said to them, "Go and show yourselves to the priests." And as they went, they were made clean. Then one of them, when he saw that he was healed, turned back, praising God with a loud voice. He prostrated himself at Jesus' feet and thanked him. And he was a Samaritan. Then Jesus asked, "Were not ten made clean? But the other nine, where are they? Was none of them found to return and give praise to God except this foreigner?" Then he said to him, "Get up and go on your way; your faith has made you well."
(Luke 17:11-19)

38

Lifting As We Climb—motto, National Association of Colored Women's Clubs (circa 1896)

Kevin Durant walked up to the podium to receive his award as the 2014 NBA Most Valuable Player. What he said went viral. It was on the Internet and on social media. It was printed in newspapers. His speech was broadcast on radio and television. From the podium, looking at his mother in the audience, he said, "We weren't supposed to be here. You made us believe. You kept us off the street, put clothes on our backs, food on the table. When you didn't eat, you made sure we ate. You went to sleep hungry. You sacrificed for us. You're the real MVP."[14]

Durant acknowledged his gratitude.

Take the time today to let someone know you're thankful for the difference they've made in your life. Someone petitioned God on your behalf. It's your time to invoke blessings on them.

Prayer Focus

O God, you are my God, I seek you,
my soul thirsts for you;
my flesh faints for you,
as in a dry and weary land where there is no water.
So I have looked upon you in the sanctuary,
beholding your power and glory.
Because your steadfast love is better than life,
my lips will praise you.
So I will bless you as long as I live;
I will lift up my hands and call on your name.
—Psalm 63:1-4

Day 17
Friday
Children

People were bringing even infants to him that he might touch them; and when the disciples saw it, they sternly ordered them not to do it. But Jesus called for them and said, "Let the little children come to me, and do not stop them; for it is to such as these that the kingdom of God belongs. Truly I tell you, whoever does not receive the kingdom of God as a little child will never enter it." (Luke 18:15-17)

Children are the award of life.—saying, West Africa

The Children's Defense Fund reports *Each Day in America for Black Children*:

Less than one mother dies from complications of childbirth.
Less than one child is killed by abuse or neglect.
3 children or teens are killed by guns
4 children or teens die from accidents.
19 babies die before their first birthdays.
86 children are arrested for violent crimes.
90 children are arrested for drug crimes.
153 babies are born to teen mothers.
173 babies are born without health insurance.
212 babies are born at low birthweight.
318 public school students are corporally punished.*
367 babies are born into extreme poverty.
399 children are confirmed as abused or neglected.
625 babies are born into poverty.
763 high school students drop out.*
1,144 babies are born to unmarried mothers.
1,174 children are arrested.

4,529 public school students are suspended.*
*Base on 180 school days a year.[15]

The children, our children, need what Christ offers. Despite the disciples who tried to deter the people from bringing the little ones, Jesus still manages to touch their lives.

This generation is facing unimaginable obstacles. They need more than a Christianity of convenience. They don't need the local church to be their stumbling block, getting between them and Jesus. The church needs penance for the manner in which it can stifle the spiritual growth of today's youth.

Dr. Samuel Proctor was a preacher, teacher, college president, and proponent of social justice issues. He used to tell the story of the time he was in Calcutta, India. He was himself face-to-face with unimaginable poverty and death. In the midst of such despairing conditions, he and a colleague found themselves in a rickshaw, pulled by an underweight boy of about 11 years old.[16]

Proctor said, "It was too much. I had to stop him, climb down, and pay him the fare, double, to settle with my conscience. I know he needed customers and that if I did not ride someone else would have to. But I could not. The symbolism was too heavy for me. He was not in school; there was no other future for him. Presumably, he had accepted that he was permanently assigned to this status in life."[17]

That little boy needed deliverance from his condition.

God's good news gives deliverance for all of us, the educated and the illiterate, the rich and the poor, the high and the low. We are all precious in the God's sight.

As Christians, as believers, we usher in deliverance for all persons, including those with muscular dystrophy, Alzheimer's, HIV, cancer, dementia, or any other disease.

Prayer Focus

For a child has been born for us,
a son given to us;
authority rests upon his shoulders;
and he is named
Wonderful Counselor, Mighty God,
Everlasting Father, Prince of Peace.
His authority shall grow continually,
and there shall be endless peace
for the throne of David and his kingdom.
He will establish and uphold it
with justice and with righteousness
from this time onward and for evermore.
The zeal of the LORD of hosts will do this.
—Isaiah 9:6-7

Day 18
Saturday
Salvation

A certain ruler asked him, "Good Teacher, what must I do to inherit eternal life?" Jesus said to him, "Why do you call me good? No one is good but God alone. You know the commandments: 'You shall not commit adultery; You shall not murder; You shall not steal; You shall not bear false witness; Honor your father and mother.'" He replied, "I have kept all these since my youth." When Jesus heard this, he said to him, "There is still one thing lacking. Sell all that you own and distribute the money to the poor, and you will have treasure in heaven; then come, follow me." But when he heard this, he became sad; for he was very rich. Jesus looked at him and said, "How hard it is for those who have wealth to enter the kingdom of God! Indeed, it is easier for a camel to go through the eye of a needle than for someone who is rich to enter the kingdom of God."

Those who heard it said, "Then who can be saved?" He replied, "What is impossible for mortals is possible for God."

Then Peter said, "Look, we have left our homes and followed you." And he said to them, "Truly I tell you, there is no one who has left house or wife or brothers or parents or children, for the sake of the kingdom of God, who will not get back very much more in this age, and in the age to come eternal life." (Luke 18:18-30)

One cannot count on riches. —Swahili proverb

It was a classic black church moment from a TV sitcom or Tyler Perry stage play. I had just finished a Holy Ghost fiery sermon celebration. The choir was rocking. The congregation was on its feet. I began the invitation to Christian discipleship. "Is there one today? Do you want to give your life to the Lord? Do you want to be made whole?" I asked the congregation.

And as I was giving the invitation, I could faintly hear the organist begin to lead the choir in hushed singing, "There's not a friend like the lowly Jesus . . ."[18]

You get it. Beautiful hymn but awful timing.

I'm asking, "Are you ready to give your life to the Lord today? Is there one?" The choir is singing, "No. Not one. No. Not one."

The comical moment caused me to consider how often society can sing out "no" to the Lord's invitation to salvation.

Jesus' journey to the cross is interrupted by a wealthy man who inquires about salvation. When Jesus tells the man about the real cost of eternal life, he drops his head in saddened angst because he considers the sacrifice too great. He wanted to follow Jesus without the real sacrifice. He wanted a crown without a cross. He wanted blessings without burdens. He wanted the good life without giving up something. The rich man is having a hard time conceptualizing a reprioritized lifestyle. There's just too much that he doesn't want to pass up. And Jesus sees this, even as he is heading to Jerusalem to pay the ultimate price for the salvation of humanity.

Prayer Focus
> "Lord, let me know my end,
>   and what is the measure of my days;
>   let me know how fleeting my life is.
> You have made my days a few handbreadths,
> and my lifetime is as nothing in your sight.
> Surely everyone stands as a mere breath.   *Selah*
> Surely everyone goes about like a shadow.
> Surely for nothing they are in turmoil;
> they heap up, and do not know who will gather.
>
> "And now, O Lord, what do I wait for?
> My hope is in you."
> —Psalm 39:4-7

Day 19
Third Sunday in Lent
The Passion

Then he took the twelve aside and said to them, "See, we are going up to Jerusalem, and everything that is written about the Son of Man by the prophets will be accomplished. For he will be handed over to the Gentiles; and he will be mocked and insulted and spat upon. After they have flogged him, they will kill him, and on the third day he will rise again." But they understood nothing about all these things; in fact, what he said was hidden from them, and they did not grasp what was said. (Luke 18:31-34)

Every goodbye ain't gone.—saying

Christian moviegoers packed into theaters across the nation in 2004 for the release of Mel Gibson's film *The Passion of the Christ*. In Christianity, the Passion refers to a short and painful period of Jesus' life in which he entered Jerusalem and which led to his excruciating execution by crucifixion on a Roman cross.

The Gibson movie starred Jim Caviezel as Jesus. And while the blockbuster movie was a source of controversy with some critics, it was a big attraction for religious filmgoers. The bloody torture scenes drew emotional responses. The crown of thorns. The lashes on Jesus' back. The blood drenching his hair. It conveyed all the pain and sorrow, but the narrative was lacking in that it never adequately presented the power of the resurrection.

In today's passage, the reality of the cross is closing in on Jesus. For a third time, he shares with his close companions about what awaits him in Jerusalem. And yet, they just don't get it. Jesus shares the brutality, urgency, and seriousness of the Passion, and yet the passion of Christ is not an event which ends on a somber note. Death does not have the last word. Jesus tells his followers that "on the third day he will rise again."

Prayer Focus
> Be mindful of your mercy, O Lord, and of your steadfast love,
>   for they have been from of old.
> Do not remember the sins of my youth or my transgressions;
>   according to your steadfast love remember me,
> for your goodness' sake, O Lord!
> —Psalm 25:6-7

Group Discussion on Almsgiving
1. What is almsgiving? What are the varied resources that

God has given us? How can we use what God has given us to bless the lives of others?

2. Discuss the interrelatedness of almsgiving, discipleship, and stewardship.
3. What almsgiving lessons can be learned from Jesus in Luke 14:25-33?
4. Consider and discuss the significance of stewardship in your church. Is there a stewardship committee? Are the resources within your congregation adequately used to address the broad range of needs in your community?
5. What is your church's view on financial giving? What does the pastor teach regarding the biblical model of tithing? What is your view on tithing?
6. A church budget gives a glimpse into the priorities of the congregation. Based upon your church's budget, which areas appear to receive the majority of the attention?
7. Consider the church's role in the economic empowerment of its congregation and community.
8. What value might there be in organizing a stewardship committee that could educate your congregation about money management, investing, charities, and consumer issues?

Personal Action
1. Reflect on your almsgiving. Write your thoughts on paper. Pray for spiritual direction so that you can best utilize what God has given to you.
2. Tithe.
3. Save.
4. Give "time, talent, and treasures" to a charitable organization in your neighborhood.
5. Stewardship includes letting go of some things. Let go of whatever is unhealthy for your Christian walk. Begin the process this week by letting go of _____.

6. Support the Samuel DeWitt Proctor Conference, an organization of African American faith leaders whose mission is "to nurture, sustain, and mobilize the African American faith community in collaboration with civic, corporate, and philanthropic leaders to address critical needs of human justice and social justice within local, national, and global communities."[19]

Notes

1. Henri J. M. Nouwen, *The Wounded Healer* (New York: Doubleday, 1979), 81–82.

2. Tavis Smiley, ed., *The Covenant with Black America: Ten Years Later* (New York: SmileyBooks, 2016), 6.

3. Ibid., 6.

4. Ibid., 7.

5. Ibid., 86.

6. Ibid., 177.

7. Ibid.

8. Ibid.

9. Ibid., 228.

10. Ibid., 202.

11. Children's Defense Fund, "Ending Child Poverty Now," accessed February 13, 2016, www.childrensdefense.org.

12. Ibid.

13. Paul John Isaak, in *Africa Bible Commentary*, ed. Tokunboh Adeyemo (Grand Rapids, MI: Zondervan, 2006), 1237.

14. Full text of NBA Kevin Durant's Most Valuable Player award acceptance speech published in *The Oklahoman* online, May 13, 2014, accessed September 15, 2016, http://newsok.com/article/4815027.

15. Children's Defense Fund, "Each Day in America for Black Children," http://www.childrensdefense.org/library/each-day-in-america/each-day-in-america-black-children.html, accessed November 15, 2016.

16. Samuel D. Proctor, *Preaching About Crisis in the Community* (Philadelphia: The Westminster Press, 1988), 97.

17. Ibid.

18. Johnson Oatman Jr., "No, Not One," *African American Heritage Hymnal* (Chicago: GIA Publications, 2001), #308.

19. Samuel D. Proctor Conference, "About Us," accessed Nov. 15, 2016, http://spdconference.info/about-us/.

CHAPTER 4

The Fourth Week
Studying Scriptures

Jesus, full of the Holy Spirit, returned from the Jordan and was led by the Spirit in the wilderness, where for forty days he was tempted by the devil. He ate nothing at all during those days, and when they were over, he was famished. The devil said to him, "If you are the Son of God, command this stone to become a loaf of bread." Jesus answered him, "It is written, 'One does not live by bread alone.'"

Then the devil led him up and showed him in an instant all the kingdoms of the world. And the devil said to him, "To you I will give their glory and all this authority; for it has been given over to me, and I give it to anyone I please. If you, then, will worship me, it will all be yours." Jesus answered him, "It is written,

'Worship the Lord your God,
and serve only him.'"

Then the devil took him to Jerusalem, and placed him on the pinnacle of the temple, saying to him, "If you are the Son of God, throw yourself down from here, for it is written,

'He will command his angels concerning you,
to protect you,'
and
'On their hands they will bear you up,
so that you will not dash your foot against a stone.'"

Jesus answered him, "It is said, 'Do not put the Lord your God to the test.'" When the devil had finished every test, he departed from him until an opportune time. (Luke 4:1-13)

There can be no peace without understanding.
—proverb, Kenya

The Holy Scriptures strengthened Jesus throughout his life. In the only biblical glimpse we have of his childhood, we find a twelve-year-old Jesus in the temple in Jerusalem, "sitting among the teachers, listening to them and asking them questions" (Luke 2:46). The temple crowd was amazed with the youngster's grasp of the Scriptures.

Years later, when led by the Holy Spirit into the wilderness and tempted by the adversarial devil, Jesus relies on his storehouse of Holy Scripture to combat and fight off every evil the devil fires at him. First, the devious devil waits until after Jesus' fasting and then attempts to attack Jesus' contextual condition and vulnerability: hunger. Jesus may be physically empty, but he's spiritually full. He quickly responds with Deuteronomy 8:3: "One does not live by bread alone."

Next, the devil attempts to capture the heart, loyalty, and adoration of Jesus by showing him the kingdoms of the world and promising them to Jesus if he will worship the devil. Jesus dismisses the offer with Scripture: "It is written, 'Worship the Lord your God, and serve only him'" (Deuteronomy 6:13; 10:20).

Finally, the devil comes at Jesus, taking him to the highest point of the temple and challenging him to throw himself downward. "If you are the Son of God, throw yourself down from here . . ." The devil goes on to say that God "will command his angels concerning you, to protect you" (Luke 4:10). Again, empowered with God's Word, Jesus quotes Deuteronomy 6:16: "Do not put the LORD your God to the test."

During the end of his earthly life, while painfully and coura-geously enduring the agony of the crucifixion, Jesus' final words (Luke 23:46b) quote a portion of Psalm 31:5: "Into your hand I commit my spirit; you have redeemed me, O LORD, faithful God."

Jesus studied the Holy Scriptures. For early Christianity, the Scriptures meant the Old Testament. The New Testament devel-oped shortly after the organization of the church. It was around AD 367 that the New Testament was accepted as the authoritative canon of Christian Scriptures.

While Jesus was a student of the Scriptures, far too many con-fessed Christians today fall short when it comes to serious and dis-ciplined Bible study. We affirm the centrality of the Bible. In my tra-dition as an American Baptist, we affirm:

> Holy Scripture always has been for us the most authoritative guide to knowing and serving the triune God: Father, Son and Holy Spirit (Creator, Redeemer, Sustainer). As the divinely-inspired word of God, the Bible for us reveals our faith and its mandated practice.[1]

Many grew up learning about the prominent place of the Bible in the black Baptist church tradition by reading that first section of the Articles of Faith, which appear in the familiar burgundy *National Baptist Hymnal*:

> We believe that the Holy Bible was written by men divinely inspired, and is a perfect treasure of heavenly instruction; that it has God for its author, salvation for its end, and truth with-out any mixture of error, for its matter; that it reveals the prin-ciples by which God will judge us; and therefore is, and shall remain to the end of the world, the true center of Christian union, and the supreme standard by which all human con-duct, creeds, and opinions should be tried.[2]

Yet, unfortunately, as Dr. Geoffrey V. Guns points out in *Introduction to the Bible: An Easy-to-Read Guide to Its Purpose and Origin*, "The Bible has become a closed book in many African-American congregations."[3] Dr. Guns, senior pastor of Second Calvary Baptist Church (Norfolk, VA) for more than thirty years, suggests four primary reasons for the biblical illiteracy in the black church.

1. The African American religious tradition tends to be more oral than written, and focuses a great deal on emotional responses to the gospel.
2. The use of electronic technology, religious TV programming, the Internet (i.e., social media platforms, streaming worship services, etc.), growing demands on the nuclear family, professional stress, and a host of other influences rob us of the time needed for serious study of the Bible.
3. New worship formats stress energy and excitement, without a corresponding emphasis on the teaching and preaching ministries of the local church.
4. Critical Bible study involves taking the time to understand cultural, historical, social, religious, political and biblical contexts.[4]

A Christian is a disciple of Jesus Christ. This means we follow the teachings of Jesus and earnestly try to live the life he exhibited. This means disciplined study of the Holy Scriptures. Concentrate on reading and studying the Bible this week. Utilize this devotional book as the kindling wood to spark a fire within you! Take full advantage of the learning opportunities in your church.

Day 20
Monday
Vision

As he approached Jericho, a blind man was sitting by the roadside begging. When he heard a crowd going by, he asked what was happening. They told him, "Jesus of Nazareth is passing by." Then he shouted, "Jesus, Son of David, have mercy on me!" Those who were in front sternly ordered him to be quiet; but he shouted even more loudly, "Son of David, have mercy on me!" Jesus stood still and ordered the man to be brought to him; and when he came near, he asked him, "What do you want me to do for you?" He said, "Lord, let me see again." Jesus said to him, "Receive your sight; your faith has saved you." Immediately he regained his sight and followed him, glorifying God; and all the people, when they saw it, praised God. (Luke 18:35-43)

This little light of mine,
I'm gonna let it shine.
— "This Little Light of Mine"

The blind beggar near Jericho really did have vision. That is, he could envision his sight restored. Despite those who tried to silence him, he was determined to receive the miraculous healing that he believed the Lord could provide. He made supplication to the Lord.

Not too long ago, I heard someone saying some extremely negative remarks about our neighbors living in Tidewater Gardens, a public housing neighborhood in downtown Norfolk, Virginia. I believe the remarks were not made with malice but out of ignorance, fear, and frustration. We've all heard these kind of insensitive and illogical remarks. It's as though the persons use a broad brush to paint a picture of wholesale parental neglect, addictions, drug traffic, violent crime, senseless murder, and hopelessness for everyone living in public housing. But just because people live in public housing does not mean they can't see opportunity and deliverance. Furthermore, it doesn't mean that they aren't working with what they have.

Luke's Gospel shows Jesus as a champion of the oppressed.

When your haters and detractors try to derail your determination to dream, you dream, anyhow! Rev. Jesse Jackson said in his 1988 address to the Democratic National Convention, "Hold your head high, stick your chest out. You can make it. It gets dark sometimes, but morning comes. Keep hope alive. Don't you surrender! Suffering breeds character, character breeds faith. In the end, faith will not disappoint."⁵ Rev. Jackson may have lost his second presidential campaign, but it opened the door for a dream realized in 2008 when this nation elected Barack Obama as its forty-fourth president—the first African American president!

Prayer Focus

But you, O LORD, are a shield around me,
my glory, and the one who lifts up my head.
—Psalm 3:3

Day 21
Tuesday
Kairos

He entered Jericho and was passing through it. A man was there named Zacchaeus; he was a chief tax collector and was rich. He was trying to see who Jesus was, but on account of the crowd he could not, because he was short in stature. So he ran ahead and climbed a sycamore tree to see him, because he was going to pass that way. When Jesus came to the place, he looked up and said to him, "Zacchaeus, hurry and come down; for I must stay at your house today." So he hurried down and was happy to welcome him. All who saw it began to grumble and said, "He has gone to be the guest of one who is a sinner." Zacchaeus stood there and said to the Lord, "Look, half of my possessions, Lord, I will give to the poor; and if I have defrauded anyone of anything, I will pay back four times as much." Then Jesus said to him, "Today salvation has come to this house, because he too is a son of Abraham. For the Son of Man came to seek out and to save the lost." (Luke 19:1-10)

Time longer dan a rope.—Caribbean saying

God is the author of time. The past, present, and future are equally known to the Lord. The psalmist was correct in saying, "For a thousand years in your sight are like yesterday when it was past, or like a watch in the night"(Psalm 90:14). The Teacher of Ecclesiastes wisely observed that there is a time for everything.

The New Testament uses two Greek words when referring to time: *kairos* and *chronos*. *Chronos* has to do with our measurement of time. But *kairos* has to do with God's fullness of time. *Chronos* has to do with humanity's timing, tick-tock time. *Kairos* has to do with God's time. *Kairos* is when God says, "It's time." It's the fullness of time. Jesus says to Zaccahaeus, and to us, "Today salvation has come . . ." What does your home look like when redemption resides with you?

Prayer Focus

    While I kept silence, my body wasted away
    through my groaning all day long.
    For day and night your hand was heavy upon me;

my strength was dried up as by the heat of summer.   *Selah*
Then I acknowledged my sin to you,
and I did not hide my iniquity;
I said, "I will confess my transgressions to the LORD,"
and you forgave the guilt of my sin.   *Selah*
—Psalm 32:3-5

Day 22
Wednesday
Hallelujah!

As he was now approaching the path down from the Mount of Olives, the whole multitude of the disciples began to praise God joyfully with a loud voice for all the deeds of power that they had seen, saying,

"Blessed is the king
  who comes in the name of the Lord!
Peace in heaven,
  and glory in the highest heaven!"

Some of the Pharisees in the crowd said to him, "Teacher, order your disciples to stop." He answered, "I tell you, if these were silent, the stones would shout out." (Luke 19:37-40)

I sing because I'm happy,
I sing because I'm free.
— "His Eye Is on the Sparrow"

A preacher shared an insightful story about the church she had been called to serve as pastor. Let's call it the New First Baptist Church. It was a beautiful congregation that had built a lovely edifice in a rural Virginia community. She said that while the people were warm, friendly, and demonstrated the spiritual gift of hospitality, they were ice-cold, rock-rigid, and stiff-necked when it came to worship.

The pastor researched her ministry context. To her surprise, the congregation had not always been stiff and stoic. In fact, its recorded and oral histories offered qualitative evidence that it had been a church that was on fire for God, particularly in worship. It was a Holy Ghost headquarters! The original First Baptist Church edifice was a small wooden church. Folk would get "filled in the spirit" and start stomping to one of these old metered hymns. The church would literally shake and rock when folk got happy in the spirit.

The pastor discovered that was the problem!

The saints got so happy and joyful that they weakened the wooden structure of the little church. And those saints promised that when they built a new church, they would not allow anyone to damage or destroy it by getting happy and shouting and jumping and dancing all over the place. Thus, the New First Baptist Church was born.

And so this church that had once been a demonstration and celebration of the manifestation and intoxication of the Holy Spirit was now under lock and key of saints who thought they were doing the right thing by putting a straightjacket on the Holy Spirit.

The stones will shout praise when we remain silent!

Praise the Lord!

Praise God for Jesus Christ!

Hallelujah!

Hallelujah for God's blessings! Hallelujah for God's compassion! Hallelujah for God's counsel! Hallelujah for God's deliverance! Hallelujah for the goodness of God's grace! Praise God for redemption and righteousness! Praise God for strength, sustenance, and salvation! Hallelujah for God's Word and God's works!

Prayer Focus

From now on, therefore, we regard no one from a human point of view; even though we once knew Christ from a human point of view, we know him no longer in that way. So if anyone is in Christ, there is a new creation: everything old has passed away; see, everything has become new! All this is from God, who reconciled us to himself through Christ, and has given us the ministry of reconciliation; that is, in Christ God was reconciling the world to himself, not counting their trespasses against them, and entrusting the message of reconciliation to us. So we are ambassadors for Christ, since God is making his appeal through us; we entreat you on behalf of Christ, be reconciled to God. For our sake he made him to be sin who knew no sin, so that in him we might become the righteousness of God.

—2 Corinthians 5:16-21

Day 23
Thursday
Tears

As he came near and saw the city, he wept over it, saying, "If you, even you, had only recognized on this day the things that make for peace! But now they are hidden from your eyes. Indeed, the days will come upon you, when your enemies will set up ramparts around you and surround you, and hem you in on every side. They will crush you to the ground, you and your children within you, and they will not leave within you one stone upon another; because you did not recognize the time of your visitation from God." (Luke 19:41-44)

If you want to go quickly, go alone. If you want to go far, go together. — African proverb

In *Crisis in the Village,* Dr. Robert Franklin wrote, "There are times when we should study the pain, and times when we should share and feel the pain. Then there are times when we should mobilize to end the pain."[6] Our journey with Jesus is heightened as he looks upon the city and weeps. The compassion comes out in tears. He's sorrowful.

The church, like Jesus, maintains its ability to feel the pain of the people. It's dangerous when we fail at doing what we're called to do. There are churches that want to be mega but not merciful, prosperous but not passionate about the gospel, contemporary but not consecrated by the blood of the Lamb. They want to be the bourgeois crowd but not the bountiful blessing in the community. These are the churches that take their cue from the bottom-line marketplace. They operate like companies and corporation, and membership has replaced discipleship. It's a corporate mind-set, but the problem is that churches are not widget-producing businesses. We're not focused on thingamajigs and whatcha-macallits. We're focused on people. The church is a community of transformation, of conversion. When the church fails to do this, it becomes a dead church.

A life-changing church is a transformational church that is making a difference in the community and the world, one soul at a time. In *Reviving the Black Church*, Thabiti Anyabwile writes: "The only force capable of reviving the Black Church in whatever area she needs revival is the Spirit of God animating the Word of God."[7]

We've got to cry collectively about some of what we see occurring in our neighborhoods; and then we've got to do something to mitigate the conditions. In faith, we've got to stand and move and march and work . . . with and by the power of God's Word.

Prayer Focus

Hear my cry, O God;
listen to my prayer.
From the end of the earth I call to you,
when my heart is faint.

Lead me to the rock
that is higher than I;
for you are my refuge,
a strong tower against the enemy.

Let me abide in your tent forever,
find refuge under the shelter of your wings.   *Selah*
—Psalm 61:1-4

Day 24
Friday
Steadfast

*Then he entered the temple and began to drive out those who
were selling things there; and he said, "It is written,*

*'My house shall be a house of prayer';
but you have made it a den of robbers."*

*Every day he was teaching in the temple. The chief priests,
the scribes, and the leaders of the people kept looking for a
way to kill him; but they did not find anything they could
do, for all the people were spellbound by what they heard.*
(Luke 19:45-48)

Ain't gonna let nobody turn me around,
I'm gonna keep on a-walkin', keep on a-talkin',

Marchin' up to freedom land!
— "Ain't Gonna Let Nobody Turn Me Around"

A man was walking along the beach on a beautiful sunny day. In the distance, he could see a teenage boy running back and forth between the surf's edge and the beach. The teen ran back and forth. He demonstrated syncopated movement, back and forth.

As the man approached, he could see there were hundreds of starfish stranded on the shore. It was obviously the result of the natural action of the tide.

The man was struck by the apparent futility of the task. There were far too many starfish. Many of them were sure to perish. As the man approached the boy, the boy kept to the task of picking up a starfish and throwing it into the surf.

Finally, the man said, "Son, you must be crazy. There are thousands of miles of beach covered with starfish. You can't possibly make a difference."

The teen stopped and looked at the man. He then stooped down and picked up one more starfish, and tossed it back into the sea. He turned to the man and said, "It made a difference to that one!"

Jesus cleansed the temple because he is steadfast in his mission. There can be distractions aplenty, but remain steadfast, unmovable, and always abounding in the work of the Lord.

"The race is not to the swift, nor the battle to the strong" (Ecclesiastes 9:11), but "the one who endures to the end will be saved" (Matthew 10:22; 24:13).

Prayer Focus
> You are worthy, our Lord and God,
> to receive glory and honor and power,
> for you created all things,
> and by your will they existed and were created.
> —Revelation 4:11

Day 25
Saturday
Assistance

One day, as he was teaching the people in the temple and telling the good news, the chief priests and the scribes came with the elders and said to him, "Tell us, by what authority are you doing these things? Who is it who gave you this authority?" He answered them, "I will also ask you a question, and you tell me: Did the baptism of John come from heaven, or was it of human origin?" They discussed it with one another, saying, "If we say, 'From heaven,' he will say, 'Why did you not believe him?' But if we say, 'Of human origin,' all the people will stone us; for they are convinced that John was a prophet." So they answered that they did not know where it came from. Then Jesus said to them, "Neither will I tell you by what authority I am doing these things." (Luke 20:1-8)

If relatives help each other, what evil can hurt them?—African proverb

The distraught and visibly shaken mother shared with the pastor that her daughter was seriously ill. The woman had few financial resources to sustain her family during what was to be a physically, emotionally, spiritually, and financially draining ordeal. The woman inquired about her church establishing a bank account to receive donations for medical expenses. The pastor immediately said he would discuss the matter with the leaders. He knew the church had to help.

The medical emergency was discussed with the leaders. A few days later, the pastor received a long letter from a member of the church leadership, outlining in painstaking detail all the reasons why the church should not be involved in receiving any funds to assist this family. (Obviously, the church could only operate in a way that was financially legal and ethically sound.) The pastor was stunned. A mountain of legalese was being used to block an opportunity to help a congregant, obviously facing a crisis.

When there's a need, let's remember that the sovereignty of Jesus empowers us to do something. With contrite hearts, let's move beyond the paralysis of analysis.

Prayer Focus

> I believe that I shall see the goodness of the LORD
> in the land of the living.
> Wait for the LORD;
> be strong, and let your heart take courage;
> wait for the LORD!
> —Psalm 27:13-14

Day 26
Fourth Sunday in Lent
Pretense

So they watched him and sent spies who pretended to be honest, in order to trap him by what he said, so as to hand him over to the jurisdiction and authority of the governor. So they asked him, "Teacher, we know that you are right in what you say and teach, and you show deference to no one, but teach the way of God in accordance with truth. Is it lawful for us to pay taxes to the emperor, or not?" But he perceived their craftiness and said to them, "Show me a denarius. Whose head and whose title does it bear?" They said, "The emperor's." He said to them, "Then give to the emperor the things that are the emperor's, and to God the things that are God's." And they were not able in the presence of the people to trap him by what he said; and being amazed by his answer, they became silent. (Luke 20:20-26)

In the moment of crisis, the wise build bridges and the foolish build dams.—Nigerian proverb

Paul Lawrence Dunbar's poem "We Wear the Mask" addresses the suffering of black folk while wearing a happy face as a survival tactic. While Jesus was not masking his true feelings in this story, he did manage to demonstrate a strength and cool and composure which one could mistake for a mask. In reality, he showed us the clarity of his capacity to remain unwavering in the face of pretense.

First Lady Michelle Obama said in her speech at the 2016 Democratic National Convention, referring to the negative campaigning, "When they go low, we go high."

In *Leadership and the Art of Struggle*, Steven Snyder asserts that "savvy leaders" embrace struggle as an opportunity for growth and learning. Engaging with the struggle, he says, will ultimately take the leader to a "better place," with a heightened awareness of themselves and others.[8]

Prayer Focus
> Now I know that the LORD will help his anointed;
> he will answer him from his holy heaven
> with mighty victories by his right hand.
> Some take pride in chariots, and some in horses,
> but our pride is in the name of the LORD our God.
> They will collapse and fall,
> but we shall rise and stand upright.
>
> Give victory to the king, O LORD;
> answer us when we call.
> —Psalm 20:6-9

Group Discussion on Studying Scriptures

1. What is the Bible? What is its purpose? What role does the Bible play in the life of the church? What is the Bible's role in the life of a Christian?

2. What lessons do we learn about Jesus and the Scriptures, based on Luke 4:5-13?

3. Dr. Geoffrey V. Guns identified four reasons for a lack of serious Bible study in the African American church (see page 51). How can the church address this "closed book" condition?

4. Discuss an instance when the church wanted to begin a project but the timing was wrong. What does the Bible say about God's timing?

5. Discuss examples of when you turned to Scripture for direction, strength, solace, correction, etc.

6. Examine and discuss apostle Paul's words to Timothy, his son in ministry: "All scripture is inspired by God and is useful for teaching, for reproof, for correction, and for training in righteousness, so that everyone who belongs to God may be proficient, equipped for every good work" (2 Timothy 3:16-17).

Personal Action

1. Get a study Bible that is readable for *you* and meets your needs.

2. Take your Bible with you to church, and use it in teaching and preaching opportunities. Record your thoughts, insights, revelations, and possible life applications.

3. Participate in Bible study.

4. Participate in church school.

5. Ask God to lead you to a Bible verse that speaks to you at this time. Embrace that passage as your life verse. It will serve as a spiritual compass for you.

6. Devise a Bible reading plan.

7. Enhance your study of Scripture by listening to the Bible on CD.
8. Subscribe to a social media platform that will send you a daily or weekly Bible study or devotional.

Notes

1. American Baptist Churches USA, "What We Believe," The Bible, accessed February 14, 2016, http://www.abc-usa.org/what_we_believe/the-bible/.

2. *The New National Baptist Hymnal* (Nashville: National Baptist Publishing Board, 1987), 606.

3. Geoffrey V. Guns, *Introduction to the Bible: An Easy-to-Read Guide to Its Purpose and Origin* (Nashville: Sunday School Publishing Board, 2014), 1.

4. Ibid., 1–2.

5. Reverend Jesse Jackson, "Keep Hope Alive," address to the 1988 Democratic National Convention, July 19, 1988, Omni Coliseum, Atlanta, Georgia, accessed September 15, 2016, https://books.google.com/books?isbn=0896083578.

6. Robert M. Franklin, *Crisis in the Village: Restoring Hope in African American Communities* (Minneapolis: Fortress, 2007), 10.

7. Thabiti Anyabwile, *Reviving the Black Church: A Call to Reclaim a Sacred Institution* (Nashville: B&H Publishing Group, 2015), 247.

8. Steven Snyder, *Leadership and the Art of Struggle: How Great Leaders Grow through Challenge and Adversity* (San Francisco: Barrett-Koehler Publishers, Inc., 2013), 15.

CHAPTER 5

The Fifth Week
Service

Then Jesus, filled with the power of the Spirit, returned to Galilee, and a report about him spread through all the surrounding country. He began to teach in their synagogues and was praised by everyone.

When he came to Nazareth, where he had been brought up, he went to the synagogue on the sabbath day, as was his custom. He stood up to read, and the scroll of the prophet Isaiah was given to him. He unrolled the scroll and found the place where it was written:

"The Spirit of the Lord is upon me,
because he has anointed me
to bring good news to the poor.
He has sent me to proclaim release to the captives
and recovery of sight to the blind,
to let the oppressed go free,
to proclaim the year of the Lord's favor." (Luke 4:14-19)

Sticks in a bundle are unbreakable.—Bondei proverb

This part of our journey to Jerusalem takes us, momentarily, to Jesus' hometown of Nazareth. It's to that place that he returns from the wilderness (after a period of reflection, study, fasting, and prayer) and is now well prepared to declare and undertake his ministry mission. The Gospel of Luke shares Jesus narratives that point toward this critical moment.

The first story is that of Jesus' birth. The Gospel writer records in detail and space the sociopolitical and economic context into which Jesus is born. We learn about his family and that they are people of faith who worship the God of their ancestors. The narrative then moves us into the temple where the earthly parents, Mary and Joseph, present (or dedicate) the infant Jesus. The parents indoctrinate their son into the faith. He relies on his parents to provide, care for, love, and nurture him.

Next, we see an adolescent Jesus demonstrating a quest for religious knowledge. However, rather than relying solely on religious authorities, he begins to grapple with his own beliefs. One day, after frantically searching for their apparently lost son, the parents find him in the temple, dialoguing with the teachers, discussing a wide range of topics, wrestling with faith matters. Jesus is maturing. He is demonstrating adult-like behavior. In fact, he tells his parents they should have known he would be in the temple, as if to suggest this man-child in faith would obviously be in God's house. Luke sums us this pericope by telling the reader, "Jesus increased in wisdom and in years, and in divine and human favor" (Luke 2:52). Not only did he develop spiritually, but socially he even experienced the affirmation of his community as a consequence of his beliefs. Young people can look at this as a way of addressing peer pressure.

The baptism narrative is a pivot point for Jesus, the young adult (Luke 3:21-22). He's about thirty years old (v. 23), a time of life characterized by making important life decisions. This is often a time of great change, turmoil, and crisis. Jesus deepens his commitment to God and is baptized. In subsequent verses, Luke connects Jesus with his lineage, thus suggesting a generational continuity of faith (vv. 23-38).

Shortly after the faith ritual of baptism, God leads Jesus on a spiritual odyssey (Luke 4:1-13). During this journey, Jesus encounters temptations. His faith is under fire and tried in the fire. Like other young adults, his life commitments are challenged. This becomes a period of critical inquiry. Faith matures in the wilderness. Dreams and possibilities are on the line. The late Dr. Prathia L. Hall was correct: "The only way out of the wilderness is through the wilderness."[1] Jesus relied on his faith, drawn from the context of his tradition, to counter and ultimately defeat the devil.

Next, we see Jesus returning home. Presumably, the community was unaware of his wilderness episode. Since young adulthood can be a time when believers retreat from church involvement, they could very well have mistaken his "wilderness" as a period of prodigal wandering. At any rate, he returned as someone who had been brought up in the faith. He went to the synagogue "as was his custom." Jesus now makes a bold declaration about his self-identity and his life mission: "The Spirit of the Lord is upon me, because the Lord has anointed me to preach good news to the poor. The Lord has sent me to proclaim release to the captives, the recovery of sight to the blind, to let those who are oppressed go free" (Luke 4:18), and to declare that now is God's time to do it (vv. 19-21).

Jesus was committed to his understanding of who he is. And when the community—those who knew him—responded unfavorably, negatively, even with hostility and violence toward his vision, he held fast to what he believes God has intended for his life.

Again, Dr. Hall spoke wisely when she said: "Follow our Lord's example, for the next time we see him, he is among the crowd, healing a man of unclean spirit, preaching and teaching in the synagogues, calling disciples, cleansing a leper, healing a paralytic. The path of ministry is through the midst of the people."[2] Like Jesus, we too are servants. Empowered with prayer and purpose and willing to utilize our spiritual gifts and resources, we're able to give of ourselves to the work of the kingdom of God.

The late Dr. Samuel D. Proctor, pastor emeritus of Abyssinian Baptist Church in New York City, was one of my homiletics instructors at Virginia Union University's School of Theology (now named the Samuel DeWitt Proctor School of Theology). He was also a mentor. He often shared the story of a time when he served in the Peace Corps in Nigeria in the early 1960s. A volunteer told him, "Dr. Proctor, you have a friend living near my school, deep in a rural area of western Nigeria."[3] Proctor visited that area with the volunteer and found African Yoruba Chief Oyrinde, who had graduated from Virginia Union University (VUU) in 1911. The chief had attended VUU for his theological education. He had studied on those sacred and hallowed grounds of VUU so that he might be well equipped for ministry in his context. This man had returned to Nigeria, settled down, and for fifty-one years taught and preached. Again, it was in the 1960s that Dr. Proctor met him, and Chief Oyrinde owned no luxury automobile, no modern plumbing, no telephone, no credit cards, no shower in his study, no custom-made suits, no designer shirts. And yet, scores of people counted on him for legal advice, healing counsel, farming suggestions, child-rearing advice, and religious instruction.

Proctor said he looked at this very old man with a broad and friendly smile and three deep tribal marks on each check. And he knew why that man had labored all those years, there in that vineyard with meager resources. He was there making a difference in the lives of others. He was there because he understood that his Christian faith was a calling to serve.

Day 27
Monday
Prayer

In the hearing of all the people he said to the disciples, "Beware of the scribes, who like to walk around in long robes, and love to be greeted with respect in the marketplaces, and to have the best seats in the synagogues and places of honor at banquets. They devour widows' houses and for the sake of appearance say long prayers. They will receive the greater condemnation." (Luke 20:45-47)

To run is not necessarily to arrive.—Swahili proverb

I was leading a clergy meeting at a church in Petersburg, Virginia. The pastor of the church said she had to leave for another appointment, but we were free to remain until we completed our meeting. I appreciated her hospitality. Honoring her position, I called upon her to offer the closing prayer before she left for her next appointment. Her response was quick, simple: "I don't have time to pray. You do it!"

Her words were rushed and didn't effectively communicate her meaning, of course! (Presumably she had remained in the meeting until the last possible moment and didn't anticipate my invitation.) But how often do we all rush through life, thinking we don't have time for prayer? The old adage remains true: "Pray as if everything depends on God; work as if everything depends on you." Prayer is a spiritual discipline for all Christians. James MacDonald in *Vertical Church* has said that fervent, faith-filled, persistent prayer is a prerequisite to God's manifest presence in a church.[4]

Take the time to offer prayer for your community. Pray for new mission opportunities. Pray for times of rest and reflection. Pray for wisdom and peace in your daily life, and pray for the needs of those around you.

Sick folk are healed when the church prays. We cast out demons when we pray. We have strength for life's journey when we pray. We are pointed toward the will of God when we pray. We're ushered into the presence of God when we pray.

Prayer Focus

Love the LORD, all you his saints.
The LORD preserves the faithful,
but abundantly repays the one who acts haughtily.
Be strong, and let your heart take courage,
all you who wait for the LORD.
—Psalm 31:23-24

Day 28
Tuesday
Stewardship

He looked up and saw rich people putting their gifts into the treasury; he also saw a poor widow put in two small copper coins. He said, "Truly I tell you, this poor widow has put in more than all of them; for all of them have contributed out of their abundance, but she out of her poverty has put in all she had to live on." (Luke 21:1-4)

What you give you get, ten times over. — Yoruba saying

Christ Resurrection Missionary Baptist Church in East Orange, New Jersey, was celebrating the anniversary of its pastor, Rev. Leora Liggins. While the pastoral anniversary is a tradition in the black church, this small congregation had never before recognized the dedicated and spiritual leadership of its pastor. In fact, Rev. Liggins, a humble servant leader, had no desire for an anniversary because she thought it was burdensome for the congregation.

I explained to her that it was appropriate to celebrate the work of pastor and people. They had accomplished much in the community, and the anniversary afforded the opportunity to be inspired by what they had accomplished with God's help. The celebration need not be a burden.

Rev. Liggins invited me to serve as guest preacher for the occasion. That afternoon I learned a lesson about stewardship. When it came time for a love offering for the pastor, the congregation began processing down the center aisle of the small church.

What caught my attention was a disheveled black woman. Her clothing looked dirty. Her hair was unkempt. She was ungroomed. She was a mess. But she enthusiastically joined the offertory procession. She dropped the small change that she had into the offertory basket.

Like the poor widow, she gave out of her poverty. She had a heart to give as an expression of her love for her pastor.

We, too, should have the heartfelt desire to give. Stewardship is a daily habit to be cultivated. At Queen Street Baptist Church, we teach our new disciples that giving generously to God's work is worship; it's acknowledging that "the earth is the Lord's and the fulness thereof, the world, and they that dwell therein" (Psalm 24:1, KJV). Supporting the local Baptist church enables it to support regional, national, and global missions.

Prayer Focus

In this you rejoice, even if now for a little while you have had to suffer various trials, so that the genuineness of your faith—being more precious than gold that, though perishable, is tested by fire—may be found to result in praise and glory and honor when Jesus Christ is revealed.
—1 Peter 1:6-7

Day 29
Wednesday
Readiness

"There will be signs in the sun, the moon, and the stars, and on the earth distress among nations confused by the roaring

of the sea and the waves. People will faint from fear and fore-boding of what is coming upon the world, for the powers of the heavens will be shaken. Then they will see 'the Son of Man coming in a cloud' with power and great glory. Now when these things begin to take place, stand up and raise your heads, because your redemption is drawing near."
(Luke 21:25-28)

Always being in a hurry does not prevent death, neither does going slowly prevent living. —Ibo proverb

As New Year's Eve 1999 approached, a wave of people anticipated that the world was coming to an end. A segment of the Christian church said that the rapture was going to occur at the stroke of midnight.

When the clocks struck 12 midnight, the new millennium arrived!

There were celebrations around the world. People were praying. Traditional Watch Night worship services were held in African American churches. Black folk got up the next day and ate Hoppin' John and collard greens. Life went on.

No one knows when the Son of Man is coming again. Jesus teaches us to be ready!

In this passage, Jesus began his discourse on living a prepared life. Have you sought repentance? Have you confessed your regrets to the Lord? Have you cleared your heart of any bad feelings you have toward someone? Are you ready?

You may have joined the church years ago, but have you gained understanding of a Christian lifestyle? How has your local church membership matured into discipleship? While salvation is immediate, we must continually work at obtaining and sustaining a consistent Christian life. Remain connected to God through Bible study, fellowship, service, and worship.

Prayer Focus
> Then my soul shall rejoice in the LORD,
> exulting in his deliverance.
> —Psalm 35:9

Day 30
Thursday
Possibilities

"Be on guard so that your hearts are not weighed down with dissipation and drunkenness and the worries of this life, and that day does not catch you unexpectedly, like a trap. For it will come upon all who live on the face of the whole earth. Be alert at all times, praying that you may have the strength to escape all these things that will take place, and to stand before the Son of Man."

Every day he was teaching in the temple, and at night he would go out and spend the night on the Mount of Olives, as it was called. And all the people would get up early in the morning to listen to him in the temple. (Luke 21:34-38)

To the person who seizes two things, one always slips from his grasp! — Swahili proverb

The other day our dog Pepper, a cocker spaniel, got into one of the boy's backpacks and found a chocolate cookie wrapped in a plastic bag. When it comes to findings scraps of food, Pepper is the ultimate gangster. He grabbed the cookie and quietly sneaked away into the dining room. I found him and tried to get the cookie. Pepper had a death grip on the plastic bag. He would not let it go.

I talked calmly, did all that dog-whisperer stuff, but that didn't work. He held on to the plastic bag with a chocolate cookie inside. Then I got his bowl and filled it to overflowing with his dog food.

Even put it under his nose, so that he could smell the delicious aroma of his favorite food. I could see it was wafting up to his nostrils. He really wanted the food but did not want to release that chocolate cookie that was wrapped in a plastic bag.

And when I say this went on for more than twenty minutes, I'm not exaggerating. He wanted the dog food but did not want to release that chocolate cookie in a plastic bag.

By this time, the cookie was no more than crumbs. He had handled it so much and held on to it so tightly that it had crumbled. But he refused to release it. He had a full bowl of dog food in front of him, but he was too stubborn and refused to release the crumbs in a bag. He was so focused on the crumbs.

That's how we can act. We focus on maintaining and holding on to the brokenness, the crumbs, the fragmented pieces of circumstances in our lives rather than on receiving and focusing on the good, powerful possibilities God has prepared for us. We don't want the good. We want to hold on to the bad, the broken, the bitter crumbs in our lives.

Prayer Focus

> In you, O LORD, I take refuge;
> let me never be put to shame.
> In your righteousness deliver me and rescue me;
> incline your ear to me and save me.
> Be to me a rock of refuge,
> a strong fortress, to save me,
> for you are my rock and my fortress.
> —Psalm 71:1-3

Day 31
Friday
Plotting

Now the festival of Unleavened Bread, which is called the Passover, was near. The chief priests and the scribes were looking for a way to put Jesus to death, for they were afraid of the people.

Then Satan entered into Judas called Iscariot, who was one of the Twelve; he went away and conferred with the chief priests and officers of the temple police about how he might betray him to them. They were greatly pleased and agreed to give him money. So he consented and began to look for an opportunity to betray him to them when no crowd was present. (Luke 22:1-6)

Evil enters like a needle and spreads like an oak tree.
—proverb, Ethiopia

Sometimes a person just gets used to darkness and does not mind darkness. It's one thing to not know, and it's another thing to not know that you don't know. There are times when we get comfortable being in the dark.

As youngsters, my brothers and I would go to the movies. There was always a cartoon, followed by a "B" movie and then the feature film. We didn't have to movie hop. We could stay in the same movie all day. But I always remember that after we had been in there for a couple of hours, new moviegoers would enter the theater. And folk like us, who had been in the theater for a while and adjusted to the darkness, would get upset with the new moviegoers who would stumble in and walk with uncertainty. Their eyes had not made the adjustment to darkness yet, but all of us who had been there for a while would get upset with them.

We were in darkness and had adjusted to the absence of light. We were comfortable where we were and didn't appreciate new folk coming in and disrupting that comfortable dimness. That is understandable in a movie theatre—but how often does that happen in our life in the world?

We can be in darkness and not recognize the light or even a need for the light.

Prayer Focus
> All day long my tongue will talk of your righteous help,
> for those who tried to do me harm
> have been put to shame, and disgraced.
> —Psalm 71:24

Day 32
Saturday
Communion

When the hour came, he took his place at the table, and the apostles with him. He said to them, "I have eagerly desired to eat this Passover with you before I suffer; for I tell you, I will not eat it until it is fulfilled in the kingdom of God." Then he took a cup, and after giving thanks he said, "Take this and divide it among yourselves; for I tell you that from now on I will not drink of the fruit of the vine until the kingdom of God comes." Then he took a loaf of bread, and when he had given thanks, he broke it and gave it to them, saying, "This is my body, which is given for you. Do this in remembrance of me." And he did the same with the cup after supper, saying, "This cup that is poured out for you is the new covenant in my blood. But see, the one who betrays me is with me, and his hand is on the table. For the Son of Man is going as it has been determined, but woe to that one by whom he is betrayed!"

Then they began to ask one another which one of them it could be who would do this. (Luke 22:14-23)

And my soul looked back and wondered,
How I got over, my Lord.
—Negro spiritual

Passover is a reminder and celebration of God's deliverance of Israel's ancestors from the oppression and captivity of Egypt. The Hebrew slaves were told to take some blood and put it on the doorposts and above the doors of the houses. That night, they were to roast the meat and eat it with bitter herbs and bread made without yeast. God told Moses to tell the people, "You are to eat it quickly, for you are to be dressed for travel, with your sandals on your feet and your walking stick in your hand. It's the Passover Festival to honor me, the Lord" (see Exodus 12:11).

Eating the Passover while dressed to travel was a sign of their faith. Although they were not yet free, they were to prepare themselves, because God promised to lead them out of Egypt.

The preparation was an act of faith. It was preparing for the fulfillment of the promise.

Israel was told that it must celebrate this day as a religious festival to remind them of what God has done. Israel must get ready for new life and remember the story of its deliverance. God was doing for Israel what Israel could not do for itself.

That night, the angel of death came through, but because of the blood, it passed over the Hebrews' homes. They had to give thanks to God for saving them from death and bringing them out of a land of slavery and sin.

If you're a believer in Jesus Christ, you know about a day of deliverance in your life. If you're not yet a believer, I invite you to know Jesus Christ, to accept Jesus Christ into your life. He'll deliver you from spiritual death and slavery to sin. And as you grow in faith, you'll understand that the Lord's Supper, the Communion meal, is our remixed Passover observance.

The next time you have trials and struggles in your life, remember how God has delivered you in the past and focus on his promise of new life in the future.

Prayer Focus

I love the LORD, because he has heard
my voice and my supplications.
Because he inclined his ear to me,
therefore I will call on him as long as I live.
—Psalm 116:1-2

Day 33
Fifth Sunday
Greatness

A dispute also arose among them as to which one of them was to be regarded as the greatest. But he said to them, "The kings of the Gentiles lord it over them; and those in authority over them are called benefactors. But not so with you; rather the greatest among you must become like the youngest, and the leader like one who serves. For who is greater, the one who is at the table or the one who serves? Is it not the one at the table? But I am among you as one who serves.

"You are those who have stood by me in my trials; and I confer on you, just as my Father has conferred on me, a kingdom, so that you may eat and drink at my table in my kingdom, and you will sit on thrones judging the twelve tribes of Israel." (Luke 22:24-30)

Everybody can be great, because everybody can serve. You don't have to have a college degree to serve. You don't have

to make your subject and verb agree to serve. You only need
a heart full of grace. A soul generated by love.[5]
—Martin Luther King Jr.

There's a short story that's often circulated in church leadership
workshops. It's the story of "Everybody, Somebody, Anybody, and
Nobody." You may have heard it.

> There was an important job to be done and Everybody was
> sure that Somebody would do it. Anybody could have done
> it, but Nobody did it. Somebody got angry about that,
> because it was Everybody's job. Everybody thought Anybody
> could do it, but Nobody realized that Everybody wouldn't do
> it. It ended up that Everybody blamed Somebody when
> Nobody did what Anybody could have.

The allegory teaches us about responsibility, initiative, and service. The strife among Jesus' followers has to do with status, but the
Lord settles the squabble by centering in on service. The prophets
spoke of the Messiah as a servant: "See, my servant shall prosper,
he shall be exalted and lifted up, and shall be very high" (Isaiah
52:13). In the Old Testament, the word for servant contains the key
ingredients of action and obedience. Jesus described himself as a
servant. He said in Matthew 20:28, "the Son of Man came not to
be served but to serve, and to give his life a ransom for many."

Following Jesus on this road to Jerusalem means aligning one's
life with his commitments and practices and priorities. Service is
among them. Jesus is concerned about the poor, the hungry, the
stranger, those with no clothing, the sick, and the imprisoned. He
is concerned about folk paralyzed in their predicaments, and he
serves them. For too many of us, our faith can become consumed
with moments focused on "I," "me," and "mine." Not with Jesus!

The greatest is the servant.

Prayer Focus
> Jesus said to him, "Away with you, Satan! for it is written,
> 'Worship the Lord your God,
>> and serve only him.'" (Matthew 4:10)

Group Discussion on Service
1. Discuss Christian stewardship as service.
2. How did Jesus identify his mission as service in Luke 4?
3. In what ways are Jesus' views on greatness and service countercultural to what is celebrated in the United States?
4. How does Israel's Old Testament experience relate to the saga of African Americans?
5. How does your church minister to the needs of the congregation? How does your congregation serve the local community? How is your church serving regionally, nationally, and globally?
6. Kwanzaa, an Afrocentric cultural celebration of family and community, embraces seven principles known as *Nguzo Saba*. The seven principles in Swahili and English are *Umoja* (Unity); *Kujichagulia* (Self-Determination), *Ujima* (Collective Work and Responsibility), *Ujamaa* (Cooperative Economics), *Nia* (Purpose), *Kuumba* (Creativity), and *Imani* (Faith). In what ways do the church's mission and *Nguzo Saba* coalesce?

Personal Action
1. Volunteer in a tutorial or mentoring program for youth.
2. Identify what you are passionate about. How can use utilize that passion to serve others?
3. Determine how you can use your vocational training or professional abilities at your church without remuneration.
4. Contact the American Red Cross and donate blood.
5. Volunteer to prepare and deliver a meal to a senior citizen.
6. Prepare and mail a box of goodies to a college student.

Notes

1. Prathia L. Hall, quoted in Martha Simmons and Frank A. Thomas, eds., *Preaching with Sacred Fire: An Anthology of African American Sermons, 1750 to the Present* (New York: Norton, 2010), 691.

2. Ibid., 693.

3. Samuel DeWitt Proctor, *The Substance of Things Hoped For: A Memoir of African American Faith* (New York: G. P. Putnam's Sons, 1995), 103–6.

4. James MacDonald, *Vertical Church: What Every Heart Longs For, What Every Church Can Be* (Colorado Spring, CO: David C. Cook, 2012).

5. Coretta Scott King, *The Words of Martin Luther King Jr.* (New York: William Morrow, 1996), 17.

CHAPTER 6

The Sixth Week
Gratitude

And he rolled up the scroll, gave it back to the attendant, and sat down. The eyes of all in the synagogue were fixed on him. Then he began to say to them, "Today this scripture has been fulfilled in your hearing." All spoke well of him and were amazed at the gracious words that came from his mouth. They said, "Is not this Joseph's son?" He said to them, "Doubtless you will quote to me this proverb, 'Doctor, cure yourself!' And you will say, 'Do here also in your hometown the things that we have heard you did at Capernaum.'" And he said, "Truly I tell you, no prophet is accepted in the prophet's hometown. But the truth is, there were many widows in Israel in the time of Elijah, when the heaven was shut up three years and six months, and there was a severe famine over all the land; yet Elijah was sent to none of them except to a widow at Zarephath in Sidon. There were also many lepers in Israel in the time of the prophet Elisha, and none of them was cleansed except Naaman the Syrian." When they heard this, all in the synagogue were filled with rage. They got up, drove him out of the town, and led him to the brow of the hill on which their town was built, so that they might hurl him off the cliff. But he passed through the midst of them and went on his way. (Luke 4:20-30)

The sun has shone on him who praises it.—African proverb

This week we turn our attention to gratitude.

About a year ago I had an epiphany. God showed me that I have much for which to be grateful. To begin with, I'm encircled with love: family, friends, and church. I'm operating in my spiritual gifts. I enjoy serving in the pastorate, academy, and community. As the saints of old used to say, "I have a reasonable portion of my health and strength." I've been blessed with the opportunity to learn, even earning a doctoral degree. I've been blessed with countless mentors who have so unselfishly shared of themselves. I've fulfilled some dreams. Needless to say, I could go on and on. I'm grateful! And that has become my word: *Grateful!* When someone asks, "How are you?" I have a one-word response, "*Grateful!*"

But most assuredly, I'm most grateful for God—for who God is and what God has done, is doing, and will do. I'm thankful that God saved me through the life, death, and resurrection of Jesus Christ. I'm grateful that I have the Lord in my life and that he saved me. I'm grateful that I can share the gospel of Jesus Christ with others.

This week we reflect on expressing our gratitude to God and to others.

The apostle Paul admonished the church in Thessalonica to "give thanks in all circumstance; for this is the will of God in Christ Jesus for you" (1 Thessalonians 5:18). It makes sense that we should express our gratitude for God's goodness in our lives. It's good to thank God for the common things of life that we see and can take for granted. Thank God for the clouds. Thank God for the rain. Thank God for the mountains and the valleys. Thank God for the sun that shines brightly during the day and the moon that shines and the stars that sparkle and twinkle at night.

Author and archaeologist Barbara Ann Kipfer began keeping a list of her favorite things as a shy teenager. Soon the list became second nature; she found herself making additions while riding the bus, eating breakfast, and even in the middle of the night. Twenty years and dozens of spiral notebooks later, her list was published as a book titled *14,000 Things to be Happy About.*

If we took the time, we could all fill notebooks when we consider the majesty of God that we witness every day.

You may have your dream job. Your financial resources may be greater than that of your neighbor. Your educational attainments may exceed that of your peers and colleagues. But if you don't have enough common sense to say, "Thank you," then something is seriously wrong.

Thank the Lord when things are going well! Jesus tells the story of the ten lepers. He healed them all, but only one returned and said, "Thank you." Maybe "thank you" is not in some folks' vocabulary. Civility and manners seem old-fashioned to some people. As I write this, our country and the world are witnessing, arguably, the nastiest and most mean-spirited political season in the race to succeed President Obama in the White House. The language among candidates is vitriolic, petty, sophomoric, sexist, and fear-mongering. It mirrors what we see on so-called TV reality shows.

I learned as a child that manners are a reflection of your upbringing and your home training. You may not have money, but you can have manners. You may be poor, but you can be polite. You may not have a car, but you can be compassionate in your interactions with others. You may be unemployed, but you can be understanding when you listen to folk.

Paul said that believers ought to live their lives in a way that is pleasing to God. The apostle wanted to see their love increase and overflow, and their hearts strengthened in matters of holiness.

With the proper and authentic attitude of gratitude, we can even thank God when it appears that things are not going well. It's no test of faith to say "Thank you" when the sun is shining. I heard a preacher say, "It doesn't create character when everything you touch turns to gold, when every idea is a stroke of genius, when every morning is the dawn of a day that is better than the day before."

When your world turns upside down, thank God! When sickness and death come to your doorstep, thank God! When hard times put you down, when bad times knock you down, and when rough times hold you down, thank God!

We can trust that God is working it out on our behalf. Gospel music great Andraé Crouch conveyed this message in his song "Through It All." He said, "I've learned to depend upon His Word."[1]

Day 34
Monday
Hardship

He said to them, "When I sent you out without a purse, bag, or sandals, did you lack anything?" They said, "No, not a thing." He said to them, "But now, the one who has a purse must take it, and likewise a bag. And the one who has no sword must sell his cloak and buy one. For I tell you, this scripture must be fulfilled in me, 'And he was counted among the lawless'; and indeed what is written about me is being fulfilled." They said, "Lord, look, here are two swords." He replied, "It is enough." (Luke 22:35-38)

If blood be the price of liberty,
Lord God, we have paid in full.
—Appeared above lynching statistics in early issues
of *Crisis*, 1910

Initially, Jesus had told his disciples that they were to follow him with nothing for the journey, "no staff, nor bag, nor bread, nor money — not even an extra tunic" (Luke 9:3). And when he discharged the seventy two by two, Jesus explicitly said, "Carry no

purse, no bag, no sandals . . ." He gave them authority and power
to preach and heal the sick. And he made it clear that anything else
they might need would be added to them, provided for them.

But now the last leg of his earthly mission requires something
new of the disciples. Their ministry will no longer be welcomed
with hospitality and generous welcome. Instead, they can expect a
need to fend for themselves—even to defend themselves against
danger. They must prepare for the hardship that is to come. They
must be ready for suffering.

Following Jesus on the road to Jerusalem and the cross does not
exempt us from crises in our lives. In fact, following him on this
road all but guarantees that hardship lies ahead. Tough times will
come. Just remember that Jesus is still the one who sends us—and
that God is still in control.

Prayer Focus

In you, O Lord, I seek refuge;
do not let me ever be put to shame . . .
You are indeed my rock and my fortress;
for your name's sake lead me and guide me,
take me out of the net that is hidden for me,
for you are my refuge.
Into your hand I commit my spirit;
you have redeemed me, O Lord, faithful God.
—Psalm 31:1,3-5

Day 35
Tuesday
Strength

*He came out and went, as was his custom, to the Mount of
Olives; and the disciples followed him. When he reached the
place, he said to them, "Pray that you may not come into the*

time of trial." Then he withdrew from them about a stone's throw, knelt down, and prayed, "Father, if you are willing, remove this cup from me; yet, not my will but yours be done." [Then an angel from heaven appeared to him and gave him strength. In his anguish he prayed more earnestly, and his sweat became like great drops of blood falling down on the ground.] When he got up from prayer, he came to the disciples and found them sleeping because of grief, and he said to them, "Why are you sleeping? Get up and pray that you may not come into the time of trial." (Luke 22:39-46)

I, don't feel no ways tired.
I've come too far from where I started from.
—Negro spiritual

I was a prison chaplain. Seven hundred convicted felons comprised my congregation. One day, a young man came by my office. He was broad-shouldered and muscular but weary and troubled. He pulled up a chair and began to share his story.

His father was a pastor. In fact, his father had been converted and received his call to ministry while serving time himself for a murder conviction. Now the son was in prison. And this young man went on to explain how he is a Christian but makes bad life decisions. He told me that nine months ago authorities had released him from prison after serving a fourteen-year sentence. He went back to his old neighborhood and started hanging out with his old buddies and resuming dangerous behaviors. Before long he was trapped in a violent world of drugs. One night, in a dark alley, a drug deal went bad. Gunshots rang out: POP! POP! POP! POP! Four bullets hit this young man. And now he's back in a state penitentiary.

I looked deep into the young man's desperate face. He should have been on a college campus in a classroom, or working on a job and making an honest living . . . Instead, he's in the Virginia correctional system, in a prison compound, worried about gang affiliations, sexual predators, shanks, and survival. And his thirteen-year old son is telling him, "Daddy, I don't want to be like you because you stay in trouble all the time."

I asked, "Brother, what are you going to do?"

He said, "Chaplain, I've already accepted Jesus Christ as my Savior. But I just don't know what happened. Somewhere along the way . . . I just don't know what went wrong. What I need to do is go back and start all over again. But I can't do it by myself."

What he needed was a strength that was beyond his own strength. "For it is [not your strength, but it is] God who is effectively at work in you, both to will and to work [that is, strengthening, energizing, and creating in you the longing and the ability to fulfill your purpose] for His good pleasure" (Philippians 2:13, AMP).

Jesus agonized regarding where his journey was taking him. God strengthened him. And he will strengthen us. When we're with Jesus, our lives change. Broken lives are mended. Those scarred with sin are saved. Folk move from hopeless to hopeful. From tragedy to triumphant. From being a miserable hot mess to being a holy miracle.

Prayer Focus
> O give thanks to the LORD, for he is good,
> for his steadfast love endures forever. . . .
> It is he who remembered us in our low estate,
> for his steadfast love endures forever;
> and rescued us from our foes,
> for his steadfast love endures forever.
> —Psalm 136:1,23-24

Day 36
Wednesday
Betrayal

While he was still speaking, suddenly a crowd came, and the one called Judas, one of the twelve, was leading them. He approached Jesus to kiss him; but Jesus said to him, "Judas, is it with a kiss that you are betraying the Son of Man?" When those who were around him saw what was coming, they asked, "Lord, should we strike with the sword?" Then one of them struck the slave of the high priest and cut off his right ear. But Jesus said, "No more of this!" And he touched his ear and healed him. Then Jesus said to the chief priests, the officers of the temple police, and the elders who had come for him, "Have you come out with swords and clubs as if I were a bandit? When I was with you day after day in the temple, you did not lay hands on me. But this is your hour, and the power of darkness!" (Luke 22:47-53)

A close friend can become a close enemy. — Ethiopian saying

Deacon Jones's words were ambiguous, yet his meaning was crystal clear. "I expect you to do the right thing," he said to the pastor. In other words, the deacon wanted the pastor to discipline the woman who had had a heated confrontation with the deacon's wife in the sanctuary. The pastor's prayerful response was to meet with both women. To listen. Seek reconciliation. Administer the Lord's Supper.

Unfortunately, the pastor's actions were not enough for the deacon. Deacon Jones resigned. He and his family stopped attending the church. The pastor felt miserably responsible for their leaving. At the same time, the pastor felt betrayed. This deacon, who had been so supportive, had suddenly become angry, destructive, and divisive.

The pastor felt betrayed, and, no doubt, the deacon felt betrayed, also.

Jesus' response to betrayal is peace. He appears in calm control. The next time someone gives you a "Judas kiss," reflect upon the actions of Jesus during his season of sorrow.

Prayer Focus

We do not live to ourselves, and we do not die to ourselves. If we live, we live to the Lord, and if we die, we die to the Lord; so then, whether we live or whether we die, we are the Lord's. —Romans 14:7-8

Day 37
Thursday
Remembering

Then they seized him and led him away, bringing him into the high priest's house. But Peter was following at a distance. When they had kindled a fire in the middle of the courtyard and sat down together, Peter sat among them. Then a servant-girl, seeing him in the firelight, stared at him and said, "This man also was with him." But he denied it, saying, "Woman, I do not know him." A little later someone else, on seeing him, said, "You also are one of them." But Peter said, "Man, I am not!" Then about an hour later yet another kept insisting, "Surely this man also was with him; for he is a Galilean." But Peter said, "Man, I do not know what you are talking about!" At that moment, while he was still speaking, the cock crowed. The Lord turned and looked at Peter. Then Peter remembered the word of the Lord, how he had said to him, "Before the cock crows today, you will deny me three times." And he went out and wept bitterly. (Luke 22:54-62)

He who conceals his disease cannot expect to be cured.
—Ethiopian proverb

For the past few summers, my sons and I have made a project of our genealogical studies. Each year we gain a deeper understanding of our roots. We made tremendous strides during the summer of 2014. We traced our lineage to a woman named Jane (presumably Porter) who was born circa 1820. Jane gave birth to one son, William, in 1845. William married Mary Adeline (1847–1933); among their nine children was Hill (1887–1958), my great-great-grandfather. Hill married Fannie Mills (1883–1981); my grandfather, Robert, was among their ten children. Robert married my grandmother, Maude (1902–1970). They had thirteen children: Dorothy, Russell, Robert, Gladys, Thelma, Raymond, Leon, Marian, Ann, David, Carol, Donald, and Bernard, my dad.

Summer 2015 we went to a family reunion in Fluvanna, Virginia. We met cousins related to us through Fannie Mills. Cousin Alice captivated us with her stories of Aunt Fannie. In fact, Alice's mother and great-great-grandmother Fannie were sisters who so closely resembled each other that neighbors often mistook one for another.

There is something empowering and spiritual about discovering one's history and being able to return to the geographic location where your roots took root. We need to remember and celebrate where we have come from.

Honor your origin.

Prayer Focus
> Protect me, O God, for in you I take refuge.
> I say to the LORD, "You are my Lord;
> I have no good apart from you."
> —Psalm 16:1-2

Day 38
Friday
Encouragement

Then the assembly rose as a body and brought Jesus before Pilate. They began to accuse him, saying, "We found this man perverting our nation, forbidding us to pay taxes to the emperor, and saying that he himself is the Messiah, a king." Then Pilate asked him, "Are you the king of the Jews?" He answered, "You say so." Then Pilate said to the chief priests and the crowds, "I find no basis for an accusation against this man." But they were insistent and said, "He stirs up the people by teaching throughout all Judea, from Galilee where he began even to this place." (Luke 23:1-5)

Swing low, sweet chariot,
Coming for to carry me home.
—Negro spiritual

I remember reading a book some years ago called *The Passionate People*. The authors described two kinds of people: "basement people" and "balcony people."[2]

Basement people are the discouragers in our lives. They may be people from our past or present, but their words go with us everywhere we go. They are the negative influences in our lives. They're the one who tell us: "You can't do that." "That's a stupid thing to do." "You will never amount to anything."

These basement people divert us from our hopes and dreams. They constantly point out what is wrong, rather than what is right with us. Basement people cause a room to light up when they *leave*. And I hate to say it, but we have some basement people in God's church.

In contrast to them are the balcony people. And hallelujah, we've got some balcony people in God's church, too. These are the people who are full of love and cheer us on. They encourage us to be loving, courageous followers of Christ. They sit in the balcony of our lives like a heavenly cheering section, saying, "You can do it!" "We believe in you!" "You are special to us." Balcony people are the great encouragers in our lives, and we all need them!

Balcony people try to lift people up to where God calls us to be, and basement folk try to drag people down to where they are. Are you a basement dweller, or do you have a place in the balcony?

Prayer Focus

    Surely God is my salvation;
    I will trust, and will not be afraid,
    for the LORD God is my strength and my might;
    he has become my salvation.
    —Isaiah 12:2

Day 39
Saturday
Bedfellows

When Pilate heard this, he asked whether the man was a Galilean. And when he learned that he was under Herod's jurisdiction, he sent him off to Herod, who was himself in Jerusalem at that time. When Herod saw Jesus, he was very glad, for he had been wanting to see him for a long time, because he had heard about him and was hoping to see him perform some sign. He questioned him at some length, but Jesus gave him no answer. The chief priests and the scribes stood by, vehemently accusing him. Even Herod with his soldiers treated him with contempt and mocked him; then he put an elegant robe on him, and sent him back to Pilate. That same day Herod and Pilate became friends with each other; before this they had been enemies. (Luke 23:6-12)

De boll-weevil's in de cotton,
De cut-worm's in de corn,
De Devil's in de white man;
An' de war's a-gwine on.
Poor Nigger hadn't got no home!
—Folk song

The chief priest and scribes are pushing their case for the execution of Jesus. The Gospel writer walks us through the hearing before the Sanhedrin (Luke 22:66-71), the hearing before Pontius Pilate (Luke 23:1-5), and now the hearing before Herod Antipas.

Pilate, the Roman governor of Judea, Samaria, and Idumea from AD 26 to 36, does not want to deal with the responsibility of deciding Jesus' case. The religious leaders are charging Jesus with blasphemy, but they are presenting their case to the Roman authorities as that of treason. They portray Jesus as a rabble-rouser, an insurgent against Rome. And so, Pilate sends Jesus to Herod, the surviving son of Herod the Great and tetrarch of Galilee and Perea (4 BC to AD 39).

As Jesus is led from hearing to hearing, Herod and Pilate "became friends with each other; before this they had been enemies." Herod and Pilate are united because of the sinister plot to crucify Jesus. Evil intentions can create unlikely alliances. Shakespeare's Trinculo says it correctly in *The Tempest* (Act 2, scene 2), "Misery acquaints a man with strange bedfellows."[3]

There are times when situations and interests can bring together those who otherwise have little in common.

Prayer Focus

[God's] divine power has given us everything needed for life and godliness, through the knowledge of him who called us by his own glory and goodness. Thus he has given us, through these things, his precious and very great promises, so that through them you may escape from the corruption that is in the world because of lust, and may become participants in the divine nature.

—2 Peter 1:3-4

Group Discussion on Gratitude

1. How do people generally respond to hardship? Consider and discuss the Christian response to hardship. What do the Scriptures say about difficult times?
2. What does Jesus do during difficult moments in his life? Give examples of how Jesus handled the particularly difficult moments.
3. How does a Christian find daily strength?
4. Discuss the power of encouragement.
5. When have you felt betrayed? How did you respond? Would you respond any differently today? Why or why not?
6. Who has been a particular blessing in your life?

Personal Action

1. Reflect on and write down reasons for which you are grateful.
2. Over the next seven days, write one thank-you note each day to someone who has been a blessing in your life.
3. Meditate on Scriptures that focus on thankfulness, such as Colossians 2:6, Colossians 3:15, and Hebrews 12:28.

Notes

1. Andraé Crouch, "Through It All," *Soulfully* (Compendia, 1972), compact disc.

2. Keith Miller and Bruce Larson, *The Passionate People: Carriers of the Spirit* (Nashville: W Publishing Group, 1979).

3. Barbara A. Mowat and Paul Werstine, eds., *The Tempest by William Shakespeare* (New York: Simon & Schuster Paperbacks, 2009), 79.

CHAPTER 7

Holy Week

When they heard this, all in the synagogue were filled with rage. They got up, drove him out of the town, and led him to the brow of the hill on which their town was built, so that they might hurl him off the cliff. But he passed through the midst of them and went on his way. (Luke 4:28-30)

With these words he went forward on his way to Jerusalem. (Luke 19:28, Moffatt)

When you follow in the path of your father, you learn to walk like him.—Ashanti proverb

Jesus has been on his way to Calvary even before he preached his initial sermon at his hometown synagogue in Nazareth. He has always been on his way toward the cross. Luke tells us that now the pilgrimage intensifies. We begin this last leg of our seasonal devotional journey with Holy Week. While Christendom designates it Holy Week, it lasts eight days from Jesus' triumphal entry into Jerusalem on Palm Sunday, to his unjust, brutal, and agonizing crucifixion at Golgotha, to his victorious and glorious rising from the dead on Resurrection Sunday (Easter). All of Jesus' life activities coalesce this week. Following Luke's reportage, we move through the "week."

Walking through Holy Week

Sunday

Palm Sunday begins Holy Week, as Jesus rides royally into Jerusalem on a lowly colt (Luke 19:28-40). He fulfills the Old Testament prophecy: "Lo, your king comes to you; triumphant and victorious is he, humble and riding on a donkey" (Zechariah 9:9b). Enthusiastic crowds welcome Jesus: "So they took branches of palm trees and went out to meet him, shouting, 'Hosanna! Blessed is the one who comes in the name of the Lord—the King of Israel!'" (John 12:13). Jesus comes closer to the city and weeps over Jerusalem (Luke 19:41-44).

Monday

Jesus enters the temple and begins turning over tables because merchants are using the sacred space for selling their goods (Luke 19:45-46). With outrage, Jesus declares, "It is written, 'My house shall be a house of prayer'; but you have made it a den of robbers" (Luke 19:45). In response, the religious leaders "kept looking for a way to kill him" (Luke 19:48).

Tuesday

The chief priests, teachers of the Law, and the elders raise questions about the liberating good news Jesus is preaching, and the authority by which he boldly acts (Luke 20:1-8). Jesus addresses several of the questions raised by the religious leaders, and he does so with his masterful use of language. He tells parables, warns against hypocrisy among religious leaders, foretells persecutions and desolation, and concludes by admonishing his listeners to be watchful (Luke 20–21). "Be alert at all times, praying that you may have the strength to escape all these things that will take place, and to stand before the Son of Man" (Luke 21:36).

Wednesday

Scripture is silent regarding Jesus' activities on Wednesday. However, "the chief priests and scribes were looking for a way to put Jesus to death" (Luke 22:2). Satan enters Judas Iscariot (one of Jesus' twelve closest companions and followers), and Judas plots with religious leaders to betray Jesus—for money—"when no crowd was present" (Luke 22:5-6).

Thursday

Thursday is a frenzy of activity, beginning with Jesus directing Peter and John to go into Jerusalem and prepare for the Passover meal (Luke 22:7-14). Jesus takes this traditional Jewish meal that commemorates Israel's liberation from Egyptian captivity and transforms it into what the church would ritualize as Communion. Jesus foretells his betrayal (Luke 22:21-22); teaches a lesson on how greatness is found in service (Luke 22:24-27); predicts Peter's denial (Luke 22:31-34); and leads his disciples outside the city walls for a prayer meeting at the Mount of Olives (Luke 22:39-45). As soon as the prayer is completed, Judas is there with a crowd of religious leaders and temple authorities who quickly arrest Jesus and haul him off.

Friday

Events move swiftly from capture in the Garden of Gethsemane to courtroom trials before Jews and Gentiles alike, to crucifixion and burial (Luke 22:54–23:53). The disciples, male and female alike, are left reeling in grief and confusion at the abrupt execution of their beloved friend and teacher.

Saturday

Saturday is the Jewish Sabbath, a day for rest and reflection on God's Word alone. Ironically, however, the Jewish leaders break the Sabbath to ensure that Jesus, God's Living Word, is securely entombed (Matthew 27:62-66).

Sunday

The dawn of the new day reveals "the stone rolled away from the tomb" (Luke 24:2), and the body of Jesus is not there. The journey with Jesus culminates with history's greatest event: "He is risen!" Jesus redeems humanity by his resurrection from the grave. He appears to his disciples and speaks peace to their terror and disbelief.

Day 40
Palm Sunday
Direction

After he had said this, he went on ahead, going up to Jerusalem. When he had come near Bethphage and Bethany, at the place called the Mount of Olives, he sent two of the disciples, saying, "Go into the village ahead of you, and as you enter it you will find tied there a colt that has never been ridden. Untie it and bring it here. If anyone asks you, 'Why are you untying it?' just say this, 'The Lord needs it.'" So those who were sent departed and found it as he had told them. As they were untying the colt, its owners asked them, "Why are you untying the colt?" They said, "The Lord needs it." (Luke 19:28-34)

Wherever a man goes to dwell his character goes with him.
—African proverb

In Lewis Carroll's classic *Alice's Adventures in Wonderland*, Alice asks the Cat, Cheshire Puss, for directions. The Cat responds by saying,

"That depends a good deal on where you want to go."
"I don't much care where—," said Alice.
"Then it doesn't matter which way you go," said the Cat.[1]

Unlike Alice, we see that Jesus moves with decisive direction. He was a champion for the poor, associated with the marginalized, healed and performed miracles—moved with purpose. He was concerned about the economic and social conditions pressing down upon humanity. His three years of public ministry advanced a gospel to "seek out and to save the lost" (Luke 19:10), illustrated even through parables about the lost sheep, lost coin, and lost son (see Luke 15). Jesus knew where he was going and calls us to follow in his footsteps.

Palm Sunday points Jesus in the direction of his destiny. Have you discovered your destiny? Do you know what God has intended for your life? When you discover God's direction for your life, you're transformed by a renewed mind.

Prayer Focus
> The human mind plans the way,
> but the Lord directs the steps.
> —Proverbs 16:9

Monday
Objection

Then he entered the temple and began to drive out those who were selling things there; and he said, "It is written, 'My house shall be a house of prayer'; but you have made it a den of robbers." (Luke 19:45-46)

One cannot count on riches.—proverb, Somalia

There's growing rejection and opposition toward Jesus.

Jesus "will suddenly come to the temple" (Malachi 3:1) and confront the unbelievable activity that meets his eyes. He looks around the outer courtyard and sees excited merchants who are perverting the purposes of the sacred space by selling animals for sacrifices and exchanging money at exorbitant rates. True worshippers are being crowded out; "moneychangers" are taking advantage of the vulnerable.

When Jesus becomes aware of the incredible situation unfolding on the hallowed grounds, he responds with anger. Anger is an appropriate reaction for conditions that are antithetical to the Christ and his engaging ministry of salvation for all: the poor, the captive, the blind, and the oppressed.

President Barack Obama demonstrated profound emotion regarding the sanctity of the church house when he delivered the moving eulogy for the Honorable Reverend Clementa Pinkney on June 29, 2015, at the College of Charleston. Pastor Pinkney was among the victims fatally wounded in the bloody massacre at Emanuel African Methodist Episcopal Church in Charleston, South Carolina, during an evening Bible study at the historic church. President Obama said:

> Over the course of centuries, black churches served as "hush harbors" where slaves could worship in safety; praise houses where their free descendants could gather and shout hallelujah; rest stops for the weary along the Underground Railroad; bunkers for the foot soldiers of the civil rights movement. They have been, and continue to be, community centers where we organize for jobs and justice; places of scholarship and networks; places where children are loved and fed and kept out of harm's way, and told that they are beautiful and smart—and taught that they matter. That's what happens in church.[2]

Christians cannot stand idle, voicelessly watching unfolding episodes of abuse, injury, and injustice, particularly when they occur within the walls of the church. It is holy ground.

Prayer Focus

But anyone united to the Lord becomes one spirit with him.
—1 Corinthians 6:17

Tuesday
Near

Then he told them a parable: "Look at the fig tree and all the trees; as soon as they sprout leaves you can see for yourselves and know that summer is already near. So also, when you see these things taking place, you know that the kingdom of God is near. Truly I tell you, this generation will not pass away until all things have taken place. Heaven and earth will pass away, but my words will not pass away." (Luke 21:29-33)

A patient man will eat ripe fruit.—African proverb

My maternal grandfather, Alexander Briggs, was an artist and respected businessman who established the Briggs Sign Shop in New Jersey. He painstakingly and joyfully hand painted billboards for Coca-Cola and Flying-A Tidewater Gasoline service stations. He produced the signs for the 1939 World's Fair in New York. His shop's slogan was "Who knows without a sign?"

Jesus would agree that a "sign" is necessary if you want to communicate a message. He used a sprouting fig tree as a sign to teach about the second coming of the Messiah.

Jesus confirmed that there will be signs declaring his return. However, rather than viewing such signs with worry and dismay, his followers are urged to receive them as assurance of the imminence of God's kingdom to come.

Admittedly, it's difficult to rejoice when we hear about examples of Christian persecution. Open Doors USA, a nonprofit group focused on serving persecuted Christians in more than sixty countries, says "beatings, physical torture, confinement, isolation, rape, severe punishment, imprisonment, slavery, discrimination in education and employment, and even death"[3] are felt globally on a daily basis. And when it comes to natural disasters, on one morning news report in August 2016, MSNBC reported a 6.2 magnitude earthquake that rocked central Italy, claiming at least 250 lives; recovery efforts in southern Louisiana after catastrophic flooding in previous weeks, with at least thirteen persons dead and seven thousand others displaced in shelters; and firefighters struggling to contain fires raging across the West, in California, Idaho, and Montana. And yet, through persecution and natural disasters, the body of Christ is responding by galvanizing congregations and individuals to support, shelter, and rescue those in need.

In the midst of all this, God is saying, "Listen up! Pay attention! I'm about to do something new in your life." Jesus said, "We must work the works of him who sent me while it is day; night is coming when no one can work" (John 9:4).

As you proceed through this most holy week, pray for the deepened spiritual sensitivity to see the signs and discern the miraculous messages the Lord is speaking.

Prayer Focus
> But I will hope continually,
> and will praise you yet more and more. . . .
> O God, from my youth you have taught me,
> and I still proclaim your wondrous deeds.
> —Psalm 71:14,17

Wednesday
Fear

Now the festival of Unleavened Bread, which is called the Passover, was near. The chief priests and the scribes were looking for a way to put Jesus to death, for they were afraid of the people.

    Then Satan entered into Judas called Iscariot, who was one of the twelve; he went away and conferred with the chief priests and officers of the temple police about how he might betray him to them. They were greatly pleased and agreed to give him money. So he consented and began to look for an opportunity to betray him to them when no crowd was present. (Luke 22:1-5)

Hold a true friend with both hands.—African proverb

Isn't it amazing what fear will cause a person to do? The writer-physician Luke tells us that Jewish religious leaders are terrified of Jesus and feel threatened by the socioreligious movement he has ignited. Jesus is concerned with poverty and the problems of disenfranchisement. John's Gospel tells us that, at one point, the Pharisees declare, "Look, the whole world has gone after him!" (John 12:19). They recognize Jesus' mounting popularity as a threat to their positions of seemingly superior piety and authority.

Fear is what caused the creation of the slave codes in the seventeenth century. After Africans were brought and enslaved in American colonies in 1619, strict rules were established to advance the concept that slaves were property and, therefore, not deserving of human rights. Among the strict and oppressive regulations, these codes prohibited slaves from gathering in groups, leaving the owner's land without a written pass, and learning to read and write.

The Birth of a Nation, Nate Parker's highly acclaimed motion picture, chronicles the life of Nat Turner and the Southampton Insurrection he led in 1831. In August 1831, Turner, a slave preacher whom his fellow slaves called "The Prophet," led a rebellion in Southampton County, Virginia, that resulted in slaves killing more than sixty people; it was the highest number of fatalities caused by a slave uprising in the United States. Because they feared another rebellion could occur, Virginia legislators passed new laws prohibiting the education of slaves and free black people, restricting the rights of assembly and other civil rights for free black people, and requiring white ministers to be present at all worship services.

Nat Turner and other Christian abolitionists tenaciously argued that while the laws sought to control the lives of black folk and deny basic human rights, they could not regulate or restrict the ultimate power source of black folk: God.

Prayer Focus

For I was ashamed to ask the king for a band of soldiers and cavalry to protect us against the enemy on our way, since we had told the king that the hand of our God is gracious to all who seek him, but his power and his wrath are against all who forsake him.

—Ezra 8:22

Maundy Thursday
Correction

"Simon, Simon, listen! Satan has demanded to sift all of you like wheat, but I have prayed for you that your own faith may not fail; and you, when once you have turned back, strengthen your brothers." And he said to him, "Lord, I am ready to go with you to prison and to death!" Jesus said, "I tell you,

Peter, the cock will not crow this day, until you have denied three times that you know me." (Luke 22:31-34)

Love has to be shown by deeds not words.—Swahili proverb

In *Turn My Mourning into Dancing*, author Henri Nouwen asked a relevant question: "Can you remember what you were doing a year ago today?" He then goes on: "For those who have eyes to see and ears to hear, much in our fleeting lives is not passing but lasting, not dying but coming to life, not temporary but eternal. Amid the fragility of our lives, we have wonderful reason to hope."[4]

We have reason to hope even when we fall short. That's what we see as Jesus and Peter dialogue, one with another on this night which some Christian traditions designate Maundy Thursday. *Maundy* comes from the Latin word *mandatum,* meaning "command." Tonight the Son of Man says, "I give you a new *commandment,* that you love one another. Just as I have loved you, you also should love one another" (John 13:34, emphasis added).

Christ's love is not swayed or deterred by Peter's moment of weakness and denial. Love transcends the moment.

It's because of Christ's love that we have hope. *The Message* translation records the scene surrounding Peter's denial this way: "Simon, stay on your toes. Satan has tried his best to separate all of you from me, like chaff from wheat. Simon, I've prayed for you in particular that you not give in or give out. When you have come through the time of testing, turn to your companions and give them a fresh start" (Luke 22:31-32).

Although Peter speaks up and declares his love for the Lord, Jesus must still speak the hard truth: "I'm sorry to have to tell you this, Peter, but before the rooster crows you will have three times denied that you know me" (Luke 22:34, MSG).

But notice that even while recognizing Peter's failure, Jesus still believes Peter will come through the "time of testing," and he can encourage others in their faith.

With Jesus, failing is not final; it's the setup for a comeback.

All of the Gospel writers agree that Peter was faltering in his faith during that period before Raman authorities crucified Jesus (Matthew 26:69-75; Mark 14:66-72; Luke 22:54-62; John 18:16-18,25-27), and yet it's Peter who will preach the first Christian sermon and see three thousand souls embrace the gospel. It's Peter who will write so forcefully and encouragingly about "the true grace of God" (1 Peter 5:12). Amid our daily stumbles and struggles, we still find hope in Jesus Christ.

Prayer Focus

And this is my prayer, that your love may overflow more and more with knowledge and full insight to help you to determine what is best, so that on the day of Christ you may be pure and blameless, having produced the harvest of righteousness that comes through Jesus Christ for the glory and praise of God.

—Philippians 1:9-11

Friday
Crucifixion

It was now about noon, and darkness came over the whole land until three in the afternoon, while the sun's light failed; and the curtain of the temple was torn in two. Then Jesus, crying with a loud voice, said, "Father, into your hands I commend my spirit." Having said this, he breathed his last. (Luke 23:44-46)

Peace is costly, but it is worth the expense.—Kenyan proverb
Howard Thurman focuses squarely on Jesus' crucifixion moment
in "My God! My God!"

He wondered had he missed the way.
Could it be true that he was sure of God
But God not sure of him?...
He remembered the Cup
And the long night beneath the olive trees.
  "This is the Cup; not Death!
  To yield the right to prove the Truth
  As if it could not stand alone.
  This is the Cup; not Death!
  Father, into Thy Hands, I give my life."[5]

It has come to this horrible, grotesque, dreadful, and yet necessary moment when Jesus Christ becomes the paschal lamb who is
sacrificed for the salvation of all humanity. He pays the price in
blood to redeem the world. Everything—the miracles, messages,
and moments together—all point toward this providential period
in history.

From Jesus' ignoble birth in Bethlehem and childhood in
Nazareth . . .

From the time he begins his ministry in Galilee, teaching in the
synagogues and proclaiming the good news of the kingdom of God,
and curing every disease and every sickness among the people . . .

From the time he confronts the elite who support themselves on
the backs of the poor . . . folk living hungry, malnourished, surviving hand to mouth, impoverished, and under the foot of political,
military, and economic control . . .

The steps of Jesus lead to this passion, this suffering for everybody,
and what social commentator and *VH1 Live* host Marc Lamont
Hill would describe as society's "Nobody"—in other words, soci-

ety's most vulnerable who are often viewed as disposable.
   Jesus breathed his last.

Prayer Focus
   There is none like you, O LORD;
      you are great, and your name is great in might.
   Who would not fear you, O King of the nations?
      For that is your due;
   among all the wise ones of the nations
      and in all their kingdoms
   there is no one like you.
   —Jeremiah 10:6-7

Saturday
Reflection

Jedus tell um say, "Wen oona pray, mus say,
'We Fada [wa dey een heaben,]
Leh ebrybody hona ya name.
We pray dat soon
Ya gwine rule oba de wol.
[Wasoneba tiing ya wahn,
Leh um be so een dis wol,
Same like dey een heaben.]
Gii we de food wa we need
Dis day yah an ebry day.
Fagib we fa we sin,
Cause we da fagib dem people
Wa do bad ta we.
Leh we dohn hab haad test
wen Satan try we.
[Keep we from ebil.]'" (Luke 11:2-4, *New Testament*
in Gullah Sea Island Creole)

At the bottom of patience one finds heaven.
—African proverb

On the sabbath they rested according to the commandment.
(Luke 23:56b)

On this Holy Saturday, reflect in silence on the long hours in which Jesus rested in the darkness of death and when the disciples who loved him sat in their grief and bewilderment. How does your spirit respond to the call to be still, to be patient, awaiting the resurrection that faith assures us is yet to come—even as the darkness of loss surrounds you?

Prayer Focus

Our Father in heaven,
hallowed be your name.
Your kingdom come.
Your will be done,
on earth as it is in heaven.
Give us this day our daily bread.
And forgive us our debts,
as we also have forgiven our debtors.
And do not bring us to the time of trial,
but rescue us from the evil one.
—Matthew 6:9-13

Sunday
Resurrection

Very early on Sunday morning the women went to the tomb, carrying the spices they had prepared. They found the stone rolled away from the entrance to the tomb, so they went in; but they did not find the body of the Lord Jesus. They stood there puzzled about this, when suddenly two men in bright shining clothes stood by them. Full of fear, the women bowed down to the ground, as the men said to them, "Why are you looking among the dead for one who is alive? He is not here; he has been raised. Remember what he said to you while he was in Galilee: 'The Son of Man must be handed over to sinners, be crucified, and three days later rise to life.'"

Then the women remembered his words, returned from the tomb, and told all these things to the eleven disciples and all the rest. The women were Mary Magdalene, Joanna, and Mary the mother of James; they and the other women with them told these things to the apostles. But the apostles thought that what the women said was nonsense, and they did not believe them. But Peter got up and ran to the tomb; he bent down and saw the grave cloths but nothing else. Then he went back home amazed at what had happened. (Luke 24:1-12, GNT)

However long the night, the dawn will break.
—African proverb

This journey with Jesus comes to a dramatic and unrivalled climax at a tomb: "He is not here, but has risen." Two unidentified men in shining garments share the miraculous and wondrous words with the frightened women who have come to the tomb that Joseph of Arimathea supplied for the burial of Jesus of Nazareth. "He is not here, but has risen."

In reporting this episode, Luke could have simply conveyed the reality that the body of Jesus is nowhere to be found. However, as one given to detail, Luke quoted the two men at the tomb: "He is not here, *but* has risen." The word *but*—a coordinating conjunction—suggests there's more to the story. There's more than meets the eye. That's what we find in today's final devotional passage.

After the bloody brutality of crucifixion, Luke offers to Jesus-seekers the background story. "He is not here, *but* has risen."

The good news from the graveyard this day—and every day—is that *not only* is Jesus not in the tomb, *but* has risen! God the Father resurrected God the Son!

He has risen! Our journey with Jesus does not end with his physical death and burial in a borrowed tomb. A thousand times, no! Our journey advances to the resurrection. Jesus is the Beginning and End. First and last. One who is, was, and is to come. It's not over. Don't give up! Hang on! Go on! Hold on! Press on! God will see you through! Our Easter faith reminds us that death does not have the final word.

Because he has risen, our journey truly becomes our destination.

Prayer Focus
> Christ is risen.
> He is risen indeed!
> Christ is risen.
> He is risen indeed!
> Christ is risen.
> He is risen indeed!
> Hallelujah!

Group Discussion for Holy Week
1. Why is Resurrection Sunday so significant in the life of the local congregation?
2. Discuss the ways in which this Lenten journey with Jesus has strengthened your faith.
3. How effective is congregational Bible study in your church? Is it mutigenerational? Does the church offer a variety of Bible studies?
4. In what ways was the church's congregational life enhanced while practicing the spiritual discipline of fasting?

5. Why is prayer an essential component of our spirituality? What was the place of prayer in the life of Jesus?
6. Consider the church's contemporary response to the poor. How can almsgiving become a priority in the local church during this era of consumerism?
7. Is gratitude an obsolete practice in the twenty-first century? Why or why not?
8. On the Thursday before the crucifixion, Jesus taught the apostles a lesson about service. What was the lesson?

Personal Action

1. In what ways is God leading you toward a deeper spirituality?
2. Prayer is not always speaking to God; sometimes it's simply listening. What has Lord said to you lately? What has the Lord revealed to you, about yourself, during this season of reflection?
3. Commit to fasting regularly because you desire to hear from God regularly.
4. Commit to almsgiving because it is biblical. Furthermore, can you see that it is needed in our congregations and communities?
5. Study and meditate upon these words of Lent:

Absolution	Humility	Passover
Atonement	Journey	Penance
Chastity	Kingdom of God	Praise
Compassion	Lectio Divina	Renewal
Discernment	Maundy Thursday	Repentance
Fasting	Mercy	Resurrection
Forgiveness	Messiah	Son of God
Gospel	Palm Sunday	Son of Man
Grace	Paschal	Thanksgiving
Holy	Passion of Christ	Via Dolorosa

Notes

1. Lewis Carroll, Alice's Adventures in Wonderland (New York: Puffin Books, An Imprint of Penguin Random House LLC, 2015), 80.

2. Barack Obama, "Remarks by the President in Eulogy for the Honorable Reverend Clementa Pinckney," June 26, 2015, accessed September 22, 2016, https://www.whitehouse.gov/the-press-office/2015/06/26/remarks-president-eulogy-honorable-reverend-clementa-pinckney.

3. Open Doors USA, "What Is Christian Persecution?", accessed September 22, 2016, https://www.opendoorsusa.org/christian-persecution/.

4. Henri Nouwen, Turn My Mourning into Dancing (Nashville: Thomas Nelson, 2001), 48.

5. Howard Thurman, "My God! My God!" in For the Inward Journey: The Writings of Howard Thurman, ed. Anne Spencer Thurman (Richmond, IN: Friends United Meeting), 264–265.